What Readers Are Saying About *Crafting Rails A*

Much of the work of Rails 3 involved significant improvements to its APIs. If you want to learn more about how to use them in a practical way, this book is a must-read.

▶ **Yehuda Katz**
Architect, Strobe, Inc.

Great coders who can clearly explain their code are rare, but José shows he is one of the rare ones. This book taught me about the way Rails works, how to exploit its new flexibility, and how I can leverage my efforts substantially. If you plan to do more than just write apps with Rails, read this book.

▶ **Bill Lazar**
Software developer, Glam Media, Inc.

Not many books have been written for more advanced Rails developers. This book steps into that space and covers totally new ground with practical techniques that can be put to use right away. Great stuff.

▶ **Gavin Hughes**
Developer

This book cuts through the hype surrounding Rails 3 and teaches you practical techniques to take advantage of the modularity and extensibility that you've heard so much about.

▶ **Trevor Turk**
Freelance developer

Now you have no excuse to avoid learning advanced Rails practices. This book gives you great in-depth skills for crafting Rails applications. You can't afford to miss it.

▶ **Santiago Pastorino**
Cofounder, WyeWorks

Crafting Rails Applications

Expert Practices for Everyday Rails Development

Crafting Rails Applications

Expert Practices for Everyday Rails Development

José Valim

The Pragmatic Bookshelf

Raleigh, North Carolina   Dallas, Texas

Our Pragmatic courses, workshops, and other products can help you and your team create better software and have more fun. For more information, as well as the latest Pragmatic titles, please visit us at http://www.pragprog.com.

The team that produced this book includes:

Editor:	Brian P. Hogan
Indexing:	Potomac Indexing, LLC
Copy edit:	Kim Wimpsett
Production:	Janet Furlow
Customer support:	Ellie Callahan
International:	Juliet Benda

ISBN-10: 1-934356-73-5

ISBN-13: 978-1-934356-73-9

Printed on acid-free paper.

P1.0 printing, March 2011

Version: 2011-3-16

Contents

Acknowledgments

First and foremost, I am grateful to my wife for the care, for the love, and for occasionally dragging me outside to enjoy the world around us. Also thanks to my brother, parents, and the rest of family, who have always supported me.

I also want to thank the guys at Plataforma Tecnologia, specially George Guimarães, Hugo Baraúna, and Marcelo Park. Without them, this book would not have been possible. Everyone at Plataforma helped since day one, when we were deciding the chapter's contents, until the final paragraphs.

I am also thankful for the time given by the book reviewers, who steadily pushed me to increase the book quality. Thank you, Andre Arko, Bill Lazzar, Carlos Antônio da Silva, Daniel Neighman, Fábio Yamate, Gavin Hughes, Jonas Nicklas, Josh Kalderimis, Piotr Sarnacki, Santiago Pastorino, Trevor Turk, Vinícius Baggio, and Xavier Noria.

Special thanks to my editor, Brian Hogan, and the Pragmatic Programmers, who helped me to change the book from great to excellent, and to Yehuda Katz for supporting me not only while writing this book but in Rails Core development as a whole.

Preface

Rails 3 is so much more than the next iteration of an excellent web development framework.

When Rails was first released in 2004, it revolutionized how web development was done by embracing concepts like Don't Repeat Yourself (DRY) and convention over configuration. As Rails gained momentum, the conventions that were making things work so well on the golden path started to get in the way of developers who had the urge to extend how Rails behaved or even replace whole components.

Some developers felt that using DataMapper instead of Active Record was a better fit. Other developers turned to MongoDB and other nonrelational databases but still wanted to use their favorite web framework. Then there were those developers who preferred RSpec to Test::Unit. These developers hacked, cobbled, or monkey-patched solutions together to accomplish their goals because previous versions of Rails did not provide a solid API or the modularity required to make these changes in a clean, maintainable fashion. Rails 3 significantly changes this game by exposing a set of more robust, modular, and performant APIs.

This book guides you through these new APIs through practical examples. In each chapter, we will use test-driven development to build a Rails extension or application that covers new Rails 3 features and how these features fit in the Rails 3 architecture. By the time you finish this book, you will understand Rails better and be more productive while writing more modular and faster Rails applications.

Who Should Read This Book?

If you're an intermediate or advanced Rails developer looking to dig deeper and make the Rails framework work for you, this is for you. We'll go beyond the basics of Rails; instead of showing how Rails lets you use its built-in features to render HTML or XML from a controller, we'll show you how the render method works so you can customize it to accept custom options, such as :pdf.

Rails Versions

All projects in *Crafting Rails Applications* were developed and tested against Rails 3.0.3. Future stable releases, like Rails 3.0.4, 3.0.5, and so forth, should be suitable as well. You can check your Rails version with the following command:

```
rails -v
```

And you can use gem install to get the most appropriate version:

```
gem install rails -v 3.0.3
```

This book also has excerpts from Rails' source code. All these excerpts were extracted from Rails 3.0.3.

All of the projects we'll build in this book should be compatible with Rails 3.1. In case we have small compatibility issues and deprecations, they will be posted in the online forum at the book's website.[1]

Note for Windows Developers

Some chapters have dependencies that rely on C extensions. These dependencies install fine in UNIX systems, but Windows developers need the DevKit,[2] a toolkit that enables you to build many of the native C/C++ extensions available for Ruby.

Download and installation instructions are available online at http://rubyinstaller.org/downloads/.

Alternatively, you can get everything you need by installing RailsInstaller,[3] which packages Ruby, Rails, and the DevKit, as well as several other common libraries.

What Is in the Book?

We'll explore the inner workings of Rails across seven chapters.

---

1. http://www.pragprog.com/titles/jvrails/
2. http://rubyinstaller.org/downloads/
3. http://railsinstaller.org

In Chapter 1, *Creating Our Own Renderer*, on page 1, we will introduce Enginex,[4] a tool used throughout this book to create Rails extensions, and customize render to accept :pdf as an option with a behavior we will define. This chapter starts a series of discussions about Rails' rendering stack.

In Chapter 2, *Building Models with Active Model*, on page 19, we will take a look at Active Model and its modules as we create an extension called Mail Form that receives data through a form and sends it to a preconfigured email.

Then in Chapter 3, *Retrieving View Templates from Custom Stores*, on page 41, we will revisit the Rails rendering stack and customize it to read templates from a database instead of the filesystem. At the end of the chapter, we will learn how to build faster controllers using Rails 3's modularity.

In Chapter 4, *Sending Multipart Emails Using Template Handlers*, on page 63, we will create a new template handler (like ERb and Haml) on top of Markdown.[5] We'll then create new generators and seamlessly integrate them into Rails.

And in Chapter 5, *Managing Application Events with Rails Engines*, on page 87, we will build a Rails engine that stores all SQL queries executed by our application in a MongoDB database and exposes them for further analysis through a web interface. We will also see how we can use Ruby's Thread and Queue classes in the Ruby Standard Library to do the asynchronous processing.

In Chapter 6, *Writing DRY Controllers with Responders*, on page 111, we will study Rails 3's responders and how we can use them to encapsulate controllers' behavior, making our controllers simpler and our applications more modular. We will then extend Rails responders to add HTTP Cache and internationalized Flash messages by default. At the end of the chapter, we will learn how to customize Rails' scaffold generators for enhanced productivity.

Finally, in Chapter 7, *Translating Applications Using Key-Value Backends*, on page 139, we will learn about I18n and customize it to read and store translations in a Redis data store. We will create an application that uses Sinatra as a Rails extension so we can modify these

---

4. https://github.com/josevalim/enginex
5. http://daringfireball.net/projects/markdown

translations from Redis through a web interface. We will protect this translation interface using Devise[6] and show Capybara's[7] flexibility to write integration tests for different browsers.

How to Read This Book

We'll build a project from scratch in each chapter. Although these projects do not depend on each other, most of the discussions in each chapter depend on what you learned previously. For example, in Chapter 1, *Creating Our Own Renderer*, on page 1, we discuss Rails' rendering stack, and then we take this discussion further in Chapter 3, *Retrieving View Templates from Custom Stores*, on page 41 and finish it in Chapter 4, *Sending Multipart Emails Using Template Handlers*, on page 63. In other words, you can skip around, but to get the big picture, you should read the chapters in the order they are presented.

Online Resources

The book's website[8] has links to an interactive discussion forum as well as errata for the book. You'll also find the source code for all the projects we build. Readers of the ebook can click the gray box above the code excerpts to download that snippet directly.

If you find a mistake, please create an entry on the errata page so we can address it. If you have an electronic copy of this book, there are links in the footer of each page that you can use to easily submit errata to us.

Let's get started by creating a Rails extension that customizes the render method so we can learn how Rails' rendering stack works.

José Valim
March 2011
jose.valim@plataformatec.com.br

---

6. https://github.com/plataformatec/devise
7. https://github.com/jnicklas/capybara
8. http://www.pragprog.com/titles/jvrails/

In this chapter, we'll see

- Rails extensions and their basic structure
- How to customize the render method to accept custom options
- Rails rendering stack basics

Chapter 1

Creating Our Own Renderer

Like many web frameworks, Rails uses the MVC architecture pattern to organize our code. The controller, most of the time, is responsible for gathering information from our models and sending the data to the view for rendering. On other occasions, the model is responsible for representing itself, and then the view does not take part in the request, as usually happens in XML requests. Those two scenarios can be illustrated in the following index action:

```ruby
class PostsController < ApplicationController
  def index
    if client_authenticated?
      render :xml => Post.all
    else
      render :template => "shared/not_authenticated", :status => 401
    end
  end
end
```

The common interface to render a given model or template is the render method. Besides knowing how to render a :template or a :file, Rails also can render raw :text and a few formats like :xml, :json, and :js. Although the default set of options provided by Rails is enough to bootstrap our applications, we sometimes need to add new options like :pdf or :csv to the render method.

Prior to Rails 3, there was no public API to add our own option to render, and we needed to resort to methods like alias_method_chain to modify the rendering stack. Rails 3 changes this by introducing a new API that we can use to create our own renderers. We'll explore this API as we modify the render method to accept :pdf as an option and return a PDF created with Prawn,[1] a tiny, fast, and nimble PDF writer library for Ruby.

As in most chapters in this book, we'll develop the code as a Ruby gem, making it easy to share the code across different Rails applications. To bootstrap those gems, we will use a tool called Enginex[2] developed specifically for this book. In the same way the rails command generates a bare application, Enginex provides the enginex command that generates a bare gem for us.

Let's do it!

1.1 Generating Projects with Enginex

Enginex is a Ruby gem that creates a bare project to be used within Rails 3, including a Rakefile, Gemfile, and a ready-to-run test suite built on top of a Rails application. Enginex allows us to move from a simple gem to a Rails::Railtie and then to a Rails::Engine easily, as we will see in the next chapters. Let's install it:

```
gem install enginex
```

After we install Enginex, we are ready to craft our first gem for Rails 3. Let's call it pdf_renderer:

```
enginex pdf_renderer
```

The command's output is quite verbose; it tells us everything that is happening:

```
STEP 1  Creating gem skeleton
create
create  pdf_renderer.gemspec
create  Gemfile
create  lib/pdf_renderer.rb
create  MIT-LICENSE
create  Rakefile
create  README.rdoc
create  test/pdf_renderer_test.rb
create  test/integration/navigation_test.rb
create  test/support/integration_case.rb
create  test/test_helper.rb
create  .gitignore

STEP 2  Vendoring Rails application at test/dummy
create
create  README
```

---

1. https://github.com/sandal/prawn
2. https://github.com/josevalim/enginex

```
create  .gitignore
create  Rakefile
create  config.ru
create  Gemfile
create  app    [...]
create  config [...]
create  db     [...]
create  doc    [...]
create  lib    [...]
create  log    [...]
create  public [...]
create  script [...]
create  test   [...]
create  tmp    [...]
create  vendor [...]

STEP 3  Configuring Rails application
 force  test/dummy/config/boot.rb
 force  test/dummy/config/application.rb
  gsub  test/dummy/config/environments/test.rb

STEP 4  Removing unneeded files
remove  test/dummy/.gitignore
remove  test/dummy/db/seeds.rb
remove  test/dummy/doc
remove  test/dummy/Gemfile
remove  test/dummy/lib/tasks
remove  test/dummy/public/images/rails.png
remove  test/dummy/public/index.html
remove  test/dummy/public/robots.txt
remove  test/dummy/Rakefile
remove  test/dummy/README
remove  test/dummy/test
remove  test/dummy/vendor
```

First, it creates the basic gem structure, including lib and test folders. Next, it creates a Rails 3 application at test/dummy, allowing us to run our tests inside a Rails 3 application context. The third step modifies the dummy application load path and configuration, while the last step removes unneeded files. Let's take a deeper look at those generated files.

Gemfile

The Gemfile lists all required dependencies to run the tests in our newly created gem. To install those dependencies, you will need Bundler.[3] Bundler locks our environment to use only the gems listed in the Gemfile, ensuring the tests are executed using the specified gems.

---

3. https://github.com/carlhuda/bundler

The generated Gemfile by default requires the following gems: rails, capybara (for integration tests), and sqlite3. Let's install these gems by running the following command inside the pdf_renderer directory:

```
bundle install
```

Rakefile

The Rakefile provides basic tasks to run the test suite and generate documentation. We can get the full list by executing rake -T at pdf_renderer's root:

```
rake clobber_package    # Remove package products
rake clobber_rdoc       # Remove rdoc products
rake rdoc               # Build the rdoc HTML Files
rake rerdoc             # Force a rebuild of the RDOC files
rake test               # Run tests
```

pdf_renderer.gemspec

The pdf_renderer.gemspec provides a basic gem specification. If at the end of this chapter you want to use this gem in Rails applications, you just need to push it to a Git repository and reference the Git path in your application Gemfile.

Notice the gem has the same name as the file inside the lib, which is pdf_renderer. By following this convention, whenever you declare this gem in a Rails application's Gemfile, the file at lib/pdf_renderer.rb will be automatically loaded.

Booting the Dummy Application

Enginex creates a dummy Rails 3 application inside our test directory, and the booting process of this application is the same as a normal application created with the rails command.

Different from previous versions, in Rails 3 the config/boot.rb file has only one responsibility: to configure our application's load paths. The config/application.rb file should then load all required dependencies and configure the application, which is initialized in config/environment.rb.

That said, Enginex simply changes test/dummy/config/boot.rb to add pdf_renderer to the load path and to use the Gemfile at our gem root:

```
require 'rubygems'
gemfile = File.expand_path('../../../../Gemfile', __FILE__)

if File.exist?(gemfile)
  ENV['BUNDLE_GEMFILE'] = gemfile
  require 'bundler'
  Bundler.setup
end

$:.unshift File.expand_path('../../../../lib', __FILE__)
```

And then test/dummy/config/application.rb is modified to load pdf_renderer just after all dependencies are loaded with Bundler.require:

```
require File.expand_path('../boot', __FILE__)

require "active_model/railtie"
require "active_record/railtie"
require "action_controller/railtie"
require "action_view/railtie"
require "action_mailer/railtie"

Bundler.require
require "pdf_renderer"
```

Finally, note that we don't require active_resource/railtie. This is because Active Resource won't be discussed in this book, since it wasn't substantially changed in Rails 3.0.

Running Tests

Enginex creates two sanity tests for our gem. Let's run our tests and see them pass with the following:

```
rake test
```

You should see an output similar to this:

```
Started
..
Finished in 0.039055 seconds.

2 tests, 2 assertions, 0 failures, 0 errors
```

The first test, defined in test/pdf_renderer_test.rb, just asserts that a module called PdfRenderer was defined in lib/pdf_renderer.rb.

```
require 'test_helper'

class PdfRendererTest < ActiveSupport::TestCase
  test "truth" do
    assert_kind_of Module, PdfRenderer
  end
end
```

The other test, in test/integration/navigation_test.rb, ensures that a Rails application was properly initialized by checking that Rails.application points to an instance of Dummy::Application, which is the application class defined at test/dummy/config/application.rb:

```
require 'test_helper'

class NavigationTest < ActiveSupport::IntegrationCase
  test "truth" do
    assert_kind_of Dummy::Application, Rails.application
  end
end
```

Notice the test uses ActiveSupport::IntegrationCase, which is not defined by Rails but inside test/support/integration_case.rb, as shown here:

```
# Define a bare test case to use with Capybara
class ActiveSupport::IntegrationCase < ActiveSupport::TestCase
  include Capybara
  include Rails.application.routes.url_helpers
end
```

The previous test case simply includes Capybara,[4] which provides a bunch of helpers to aid integration testing, and the test includes our application URL helpers. The reason we chose to create our own Active-Support::IntegrationCase instead of using ActionController::IntegrationTest provided by Rails is in line with Capybara philosophy, which we will discuss in later chapters.

Finally, note that both test files require test/test_helper.rb, which is the file responsible for loading our application and configuring our testing environment. With our gem skeleton created and a green test suite, we can start writing our first custom renderer.

---

4.   https://github.com/jnicklas/capybara

1.2 Writing the Renderer

At the beginning of this chapter, we briefly discussed the render method and a few options it accepts, but we haven't formally described what a *renderer* is.

A renderer is nothing more than a hook exposed by the render method to customize its behavior. Adding our own renderer to Rails is quite simple. Let's take a look at the :xml renderer in Rails source code as an example:

`rails/actionpack/lib/action_controller/metal/renderers.rb`

```
add :xml do |xml, options|
  self.content_type ||= Mime::XML
  self.response_body = xml.respond_to?(:to_xml) ? xml.to_xml(options) : xml
end
```

So, whenever we invoke the following method in our application:

```
render :xml => @post
```

it will invoke the block given to the :xml renderer. The local variable xml inside the block points to the @post object, and the other options given to render will be available in the options variable. In this case, since the method was called without any extra options, it's an empty hash.

In the following sections, we want to add a :pdf renderer that creates a PDF file from a given template and sends it to the client with the appropriate headers. The value given to the :pdf option should be the name of the file to be sent. The following is an example of the API we want to provide:

```
render :pdf => "contents", :template => "path/to/template"
```

Although Rails knows how to render templates and send files to the client, it does not know how to handle PDF files. For this, we will use Prawn.

Playing with Prawn

Prawn[5] is a PDF-writing library for Ruby. We can install it as a gem with the following command:

```
gem install prawn -v=0.8.4
```

---

5. https://github.com/sandal/prawn

Let's test this by opening irb and creating a simple PDF file:

```ruby
require 'rubygems'
require 'prawn'
pdf = Prawn::Document.new
pdf.text("A PDF in four lines of code")
pdf.render_file("recipes.pdf")
```

Exit irb, and you can see a PDF file in the directory in which you started the irb session. Prawn provides its own syntax to create PDFs, and although this gives us a flexible API, the drawback is that it cannot create PDF from HTML files.

Code in Action

With Prawn installed, we are ready to develop our renderer. Let's add prawn as a dependency to our Gemfile:

`pdf_renderer/1_first_test/Gemfile`

```ruby
gem "prawn", "0.8.4"
```

After installing the dependencies and before writing the code, let's write some tests first. Since we have a dummy application at test/dummy, we can create controllers as in an actual Rails application and use them to test the complete request stack. Let's call the controller used in our tests HomeController and add the following contents:

`pdf_renderer/1_first_test/test/dummy/app/controllers/home_controller.rb`

```ruby
class HomeController < ApplicationController
  def index
    respond_to do |format|
      format.html
      format.pdf { render :pdf => "contents" }
    end
  end
end
```

Now let's create both HTML and PDF views for the index action:

`pdf_renderer/1_first_test/test/dummy/app/views/home/index.html.erb`

```erb
<p>Hey, you can download the pdf for this page by clicking the link below:</p>
<p><%= link_to "PDF", home_path("pdf") %></p>
```

`pdf_renderer/1_first_test/test/dummy/app/views/home/index.pdf.erb`

```erb
This is your new PDF content.
```

The HTML view only contains a link pointing to the PDF download. Finally, let's add a route for the index action:

`pdf_renderer/1_first_test/test/dummy/config/routes.rb`

```ruby
Dummy::Application.routes.draw do
  match "/home(.:format)", :to => "home#index", :as => :home
end
```

Now let's write an integration test that verifies a PDF is in fact being returned when we click the PDF link at /home:

`pdf_renderer/1_first_test/test/integration/navigation_test.rb`

```ruby
require 'test_helper'

class NavigationTest < ActiveSupport::IntegrationCase
  test 'pdf request sends a pdf as file' do
    visit home_path
    click_link 'PDF'

    assert_equal 'binary', headers['Content-Transfer-Encoding']
    assert_equal 'attachment; filename="contents.pdf"',
      headers['Content-Disposition']
    assert_equal 'application/pdf', headers['Content-Type']
    assert_match /Prawn/, page.body
  end

  protected

  def headers
    page.response_headers
  end
end
```

The test inherits from ActiveSupport::IntegrationCase and uses a few helpers defined in Capybara, such as visit and click_link, providing a clean and easy-to-read DSL to our integration tests. The test uses the headers to assert that a binary-encoded PDF file was sent as an attachment, including the expected filename, and although we cannot assert anything about the PDF body since it's encoded, we can at least assert that it was generated by Prawn. Let's run our test with rake test and watch it fail:

```
1) Error:
test_pdf_request_sends_a_pdf_as_file(NavigationTest):
NameError: uninitialized constant Mime::PDF
    app/controllers/home_controller.rb:5:in `index'
    app/controllers/home_controller.rb:3:in `index'
```

The test fails because we are calling format.pdf in our controller, but Rails does not know anything about PDF MIME types. To find out what formats Rails 3 supports by default, let's take a quick look at the Rails source code:

```
rails/actionpack/lib/action_dispatch/http/mime_types.rb
```

```ruby
# Build list of Mime types for HTTP responses
# http://www.iana.org/assignments/media-types/

Mime::Type.register "text/html", :html, %w( application/xhtml+xml ), %w( xhtml )
Mime::Type.register "text/plain", :text, [], %w(txt)
Mime::Type.register "text/javascript", :js,
  %w( application/javascript application/x-javascript )
Mime::Type.register "text/css", :css
Mime::Type.register "text/calendar", :ics
Mime::Type.register "text/csv", :csv
Mime::Type.register "application/xml", :xml, %w( text/xml application/x-xml )
Mime::Type.register "application/rss+xml", :rss
Mime::Type.register "application/atom+xml", :atom
Mime::Type.register "application/x-yaml", :yaml, %w( text/yaml )

Mime::Type.register "multipart/form-data", :multipart_form
Mime::Type.register "application/x-www-form-urlencoded", :url_encoded_form

# http://www.ietf.org/rfc/rfc4627.txt
# http://www.json.org/JSONRequest.html
Mime::Type.register "application/json", :json,
  %w( text/x-json application/jsonrequest )

# Create Mime::ALL but do not add it to the SET.
Mime::ALL = Mime::Type.new("*/*", :all, [])
```

Because no PDF format is defined, we need to add one. Let's start by writing some unit tests in the test/pdf_renderer_test.rb file and removing the existing test in the file because it has nothing to add. The test file will look like the following:

```
pdf_renderer/2_adding_mime/test/pdf_renderer_test.rb
```

```ruby
require 'test_helper'
class PdfRendererTest < ActiveSupport::TestCase
  test "pdf mime type" do
    assert_equal :pdf, Mime::PDF.to_sym
    assert_equal "application/pdf", Mime::PDF.to_s
  end
end
```

The test makes two assertions that ensures whenever format.pdf is called, it will retrieve the Mime::PDF type and then set "application/pdf" as the response content type. To make this test pass, let's register the pdf MIME type at lib/pdf_renderer.rb:

```
pdf_renderer/2_adding_mime/lib/pdf_renderer.rb
```

```ruby
require "action_controller"
Mime::Type.register "application/pdf", :pdf
```

The previous code ensures that Action Controller was already loaded and then registers Mime::PDF, making our unit test pass. However, when we run the integration test again, it still fails but for a different reason:

```
1) Failure:
test_pdf_request_sends_a_pdf_as_file(NavigationTest)
  <"binary"> expected but was
  <nil>.
```

The test fails because no header was sent. This is expected since we still haven't implemented our renderer. So, let's write it in a few lines of code inside lib/pdf_renderer.rb:

pdf_renderer/3_final/lib/pdf_renderer.rb

```ruby
require "action_controller"
Mime::Type.register "application/pdf", :pdf

require "prawn"
ActionController::Renderers.add :pdf do |filename, options|
  pdf = Prawn::Document.new
  pdf.text render_to_string(options)
  send_data(pdf.render, :filename => "#{filename}.pdf",
    :type => "application/pdf", :disposition => "attachment")
end
```

And that's it! In this code block, we create a new PDF document, add some text to it, and send the PDF using the send_data method available in Rails. We can now run the tests and watch them pass! You can also go to test/dummy, start the server with bundle exec rails server, and test it by yourself by accessing http://localhost:3000/home and clicking the link.

Although send_data is a public Rails method and has been available since the first Rails versions, you might not have heard about the render_to_string method. To better understand it, let's take a look at the Rails rendering process as a whole.

1.3   Understanding Rails Rendering Stack

Versions of Rails before Rails 3 had a lot of code duplication between Action Mailer and Action Controller because both have several features in common, such as template rendering, helpers, and layouts.

In Rails 3 those shared responsibilities are centralized in Abstract Controller, which both Action Mailer and Action Controller use as their foundation. Abstract Controller also allows us to cherry-pick exactly the features we want. For instance, if we want an object to have basic

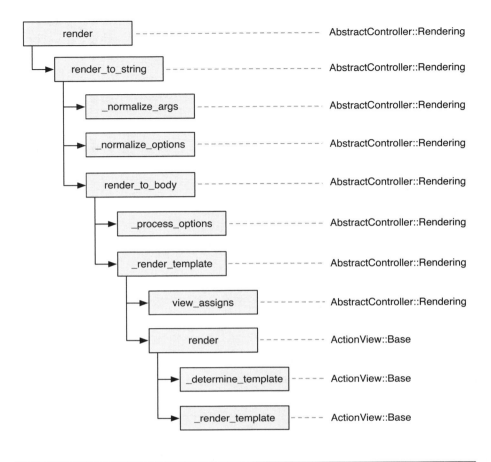

Figure 1.1: VISUALIZATION OF THE RENDERING STACK WHEN WE CALL RENDER WITH ABSTRACTCONTROLLER::RENDERING

rendering capabilities, where it simply renders a template but does not include a layout, we just need to include AbstractController::Rendering in our object.

When we include AbstractController::Rendering in an object, every time we call render, the rendering stack proceeds as in Figure 1.1.

Each rectangle represents a method, followed by the classes that implement it on the right. The arrows represent method calls. In this case, render calls the render_to_string method, which calls three methods, respectively: _normalize_args, _normalize_options, and render_to_body. This can be confirmed by looking at both render and render_to_string implementations in Rails source code:

`rails/actionpack/lib/abstract_controller/rendering.rb`

```ruby
def render(*args, &block)
  self.response_body = render_to_string(*args, &block)
end

def render_to_string(*args, &block)
  options = _normalize_args(*args, &block)
  _normalize_options(options)
  render_to_body(options)
end
```

Abstract Controller's rendering stack is responsible for normalizing the arguments and options given by you and converting them to a hash of options that complies with the public API defined by ActionView::Base# render. Each method in the stack (shown in Figure 1.1, on the preceding page) plays a specific role under this overall responsibility. These methods can be either private (starting with an underscore) or part of the public API.

The first relevant method in the stack is _normalize_args, and it converts the arguments provided by the user into a hash. This allows the render method to be invoked as render(:new), which is converted by _normalize_args to render(:action => "new"). The hash returned by _normalize_args is then further normalized by _normalize_options. There is not much normalization happening inside AbstractController::Rendering#_normalize_options since it's the basic module, but it does convert render(:partial => true) calls to render(:partial => action_name). So, whenever you give :partial => true in a show action, the view will actually receive :partial => "show".

After normalization, render_to_body is invoked. We can say that this is where the actual rendering starts to take place. The first step is to process all options that are meaningless to the view, using the _process_options method. Although AbstractController::Rendering#_process_options is an empty method, we can look into ActionController::Rendering#_process_options for a handful of examples about what to do in this method. For instance, in controllers we are allowed to invoke the following:

```ruby
render :template => "shared/not_authenticated", :status => 401
```

Here the :status option is meaningless to views, since status refers to the HTTP response status. So, it's ActionController::Rendering#_process_options's responsibility to intercept and handle this option and many others.

After options processing, _render_template is invoked, and it creates an instance of ActionView::Base called view_context, passing in the view_assigns, and then calls render on it. If you are not familiar with the term *assigns*, it references the group of variables available in the controller that will be accessible in the view. By default, whenever you set an instance variable in your controller as @posts = Post.all, @posts is marked as an *assign* and will also be available in views.

At this point, it's important to note the inversion of concerns that happened between Rails 2.3 and Rails 3.0. In the former, the view was responsible for retrieving assigns from the controller, while in the latter, the controller *tells* the view which assigns to use.

Imagine that we want a controller that does not send any assigns to the view. In Rails 2.3, since the view automatically pulls in all instance variables from controllers, to achieve that, we should either stop using instance variables in our controller or be sure to remove all instance variables before rendering a template. In Rails 3, since this responsibility is now in the controller, we just need to overwrite the view_assigns method to return an empty hash:

```
class UsersController < ApplicationController
  protected
  def view_assigns
    {}
  end
end
```

After it assigns evaluation, the render view method is invoked, and it breaks down into two main steps: _determine_template and _render_template. The former is responsible for finding the template, depending on the normalized options, and handing it to the latter so the template is finally rendered.

This modular and well-defined stack allows anyone to hook into the rendering process and add their own features. This is what happens when we include AbstractController::Layouts in our object. The rendering stack is extended as exhibited in Figure 1.2, on the facing page.

AbstractController::Layouts simply overrides _normalize_options to include the :layout option based on the value configured by the developer at the controller class level. Action Controller further extends the Abstract Controller rendering stack, adding and processing options that makes sense only in the controller scope. Those extensions are broken into three main modules:

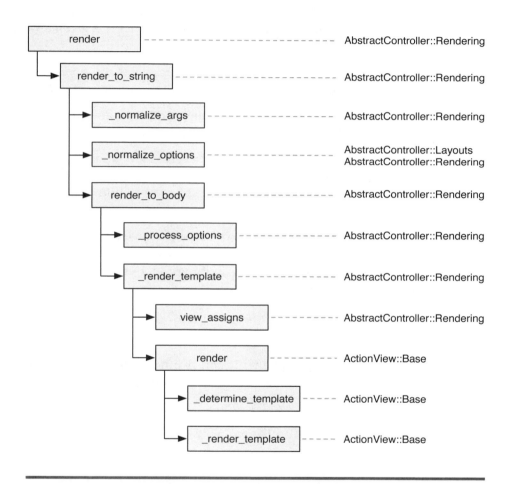

Figure 1.2: Visualization of the rendering stack when we call render with AbstractController::Rendering and AbstractController::Layouts

- ActionController::Rendering: Overrides render to check whenever it's called twice, raising a DoubleRenderError, and also overrides _process_options to handle options such as :location, :status, and :content_type

- ActionController::Renderers: Adds the API we used in this chapter, which allows us to trigger a specific behavior whenever a given key (like :pdf) is supplied

- ActionController::Instrumentation: Overloads the render method so it can measure how much time was spent in the rendering stack

The final stack with both Abstract Controller and Action Controller modules is shown in Figure 1.3, on the next page.

At first, it seems there are no differences between render and render_to_string, but when we analyze the whole rendering stack, we can see that some Action Controller modules overload render to add additional behavior while leaving render_to_string alone.

For instance, by using render_to_string in our renderer, we ensure instrumentation events defined by ActionController::Instrumentation won't be triggered twice and that it won't raise a double render error, since both were added only to the render method.

1.4 Taking It to the Next Level

Going back to our renderer implementation, we now fully understand what happens when we add the following line to our controllers:

```
format.pdf { render :pdf => "contents" }
```

Internally, it becomes the following:

```
pdf.text render_to_string({})
```

And when we invoke render_to_string with an empty hash, the _normalize_options method in the rendering stack detects the empty hash and changes it to render the template with the same name as the current action. At the end, render_to_string({}) is simply calling render :template => "#{controller_name}/#{action_name}" in the view object.

The fact that our renderer forwards the given options to the render_to_string method allows us to also use the following syntax:

```
render :pdf => "contents", :template => "path/to/template"
```

And internally, it's the same as the following:

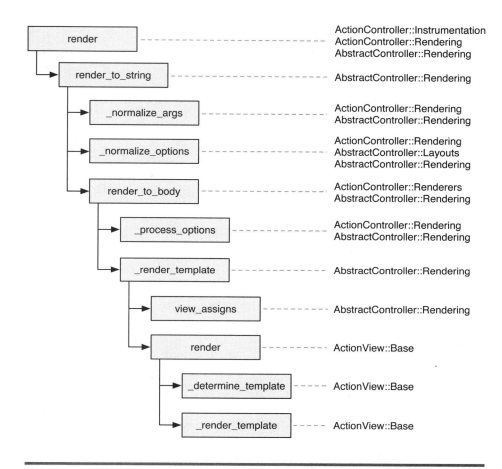

Figure 1.3: VISUALIZATION OF THE RENDERING STACK WHEN WE CALL RENDER WITH ABSTRACTCONTROLLER AND ACTIONCONTROLLER

```
pdf.text render_to_string(:template => "path/to/template")
```

which is sent straight to the view.

To finish this renderer, let's add a test ensuring this is exactly what happens! Our test invokes a new action in HomeController that calls render with both :pdf and :template options:

pdf_renderer/3_final/test/dummy/app/controllers/home_controller.rb

```ruby
def another
  render :pdf => "contents", :template => "home/index"
end
```

Let's add a route for this new action:

`pdf_renderer/3_final/test/dummy/config/routes.rb`

```ruby
match "/another(.:format)", :to => "home#another", :as => :another
```

Our test simply accesses "/another.pdf" and ensures a PDF is being returned:

`pdf_renderer/3_final/test/integration/navigation_test.rb`

```ruby
test 'pdf renderer uses the specified template' do
  visit '/another.pdf'
  assert_equal 'binary', headers['Content-Transfer-Encoding']
  assert_equal 'attachment; filename="contents.pdf"',
    headers['Content-Disposition']
  assert_equal 'application/pdf', headers['Content-Type']
  assert_match /Prawn/, page.body
end
```

Now run the tests and watch them pass once again!

1.5 Wrapping Up

In this chapter we created a renderer for the PDF format. Using these ideas, you can easily create renderers for formats such as PDF, CSV, and ATOM and encapsulate any logic specific to your application in a renderer as well. You could even create a wrapper for other PDF libraries that are actually able to convert HTML files to PDF, such as the paid Prince XML[6] library or the open source Flying Saucer,[7] which is written in Java but easily accessible through JRuby.[8]

We also discussed the Rails rendering stack and its modularity. Since Rails itself relies on this well-defined stack to extend Action Controller and Action Mailer, this API is by consequence more robust because it was battle-tested by Rails' own features and different use cases. As we will see in the chapters that follow, this was a common practice while designing most of the new Rails 3 APIs.

Rails' renderers open several possibilities to extend your rendering stack. But as any other powerful tool, remember to use it wisely.

Next, let's take a look at Active Model and its modules and create a Rails extension that can be used in Rails controllers and views.

---

6. http://www.princexml.com/
7. http://xhtmlrenderer.dev.java.net/
8. http://jruby.org/

In this chapter, we'll see

- Active Model and its modules
- How to make an object comply with the Active Model API required by Rails
- Rails' validators and Ruby constant lookup

Chapter 2

Building Models with Active Model

One of the Rails 3 features that stands out compared to previous versions is *modularity*. In the previous chapter, we talked briefly about Abstract Controller and how it reduced code duplication in the Rails source code since it's decoupled from both Action Mailer and Action Controller.

Now let's look at Active Model. Similar to Abstract Controller, Active Model was created to hold the behavior shared between Active Record and Active Resource in modules that can be cherry-picked at will. It's also responsible for defining the API required by Rails controllers and views, so any other ORM can use Active Model to ensure Rails behaves exactly as it would with Active Record.

To explore this feature, let's write a gem called *Mail Form* that will be used in our controllers and views. Mail Form will receive a hash of parameters sent by a POST request, validate them, and email them to a specified email address. This abstraction will allow us to create fully functional contact forms in just a couple of minutes!

2.1 Creating Our Model

Mail Form objects belong to the models part in the MVC architecture because they receive the information sent through a form in the controller and deliver it to a recipient specified by the business model. Let's design Mail Form like Active Record. We'll provide a class named MailForm::Base that contains the most common features we expect in a model, such as the ability to specify attributes and seamless integration with Rails forms. As we did in the previous chapter, let's use enginex to create our new gem:

```
enginex mail_form
```

Our first feature is to implement a class method called attributes that allows a developer to specify which attributes the Mail Form object contains. Let's create a model inside test/fixtures/sample_mail.rb as a fixture to use in our tests:

mail_form/1_accessors/test/fixtures/sample_mail.rb

```
class SampleMail < MailForm::Base
  attributes :name, :email
end
```

And then add a test to ensure the defined attributes name and email are available as accessors in the Mail Form object:

mail_form/1_accessors/test/mail_form_test.rb

```
require 'test_helper'
require 'fixtures/sample_mail'

class MailFormTest < ActiveSupport::TestCase
  test 'sample mail has name and email as attributes' do
    sample = SampleMail.new
    sample.name = "User"
    assert_equal "User", sample.name
    sample.email = "user@example.com"
    assert_equal "user@example.com", sample.email
  end
end
```

When we run the test suite with rake test, it fails because MailForm::Base is not defined yet. Let's define it in lib/mail_form/base.rb and write the attributes method implementation:

mail_form/1_accessors/lib/mail_form/base.rb

```
module MailForm
  class Base
    def self.attributes(*names)
      attr_accessor *names
    end
  end
end
```

Our implementation delegates the creation of attributes to attr_accessor. Before we run our test suite again, we need to ensure that MailForm::Base is loaded. One option would be to explicitly require "mail_form/base" in lib/mail_form.rb. However, we are going to use Ruby's autoload instead:

`mail_form/1_accessors/lib/mail_form.rb`
```ruby
module MailForm
  autoload :Base, "mail_form/base"
end
```

autoload allows us to lazily load a class when it is first referenced. So when we want to load MailForm, we annotate that it has a constant called Base defined in mail_form/base.rb. When MailForm::Base is referenced for the first time, Ruby loads the mail_form/base.rb file. This is frequently used in Ruby extensions and Rails itself to allow a fast booting process, because it does not need to load everything up front.

With autoload in place, our first test passes. We have a simple model with attributes, but so far, we haven't used Active Model's goodness. Let's do that now.

Adding Attribute Methods

ActiveModel::AttributeMethods is a module that tracks all defined attributes, allowing us to add a common behavior to all of them. Let's use it to dynamically define clear_ methods for all attributes. If our fixture has both name and email attributes, we can use ActiveModel::AttributeMethods to define clear_name and clear_email without duplicating code. The following test specifies exactly how these methods should work:

`mail_form/2_attribute_prefix/test/mail_form_test.rb`
```ruby
test 'sample mail can clear attributes using clear_ prefix' do
  sample = SampleMail.new
  sample.name  = "User"
  sample.email = "user@example.com"
  assert_equal "User", sample.name
  assert_equal "user@example.com", sample.email
  sample.clear_name
  sample.clear_email
  assert_nil sample.name
  assert_nil sample.email
end
```

The clear_name and clear_email methods simply set the attribute value back to nil. Let's define these methods dynamically with ActiveModel::AttributeMethods in four steps, all outlined in our new MailForm::Base implementation shown here:

`mail_form/2_attribute_prefix/lib/mail_form/base.rb`

```ruby
module MailForm
  class Base

    include ActiveModel::AttributeMethods  # 1) attribute methods behavior

    attribute_method_prefix 'clear_'        # 2) clear_ is attribute prefix

    def self.attributes(*names)
      attr_accessor *names

      # 3) Ask to define the prefix methods for the given attributes names
      define_attribute_methods names
    end

    protected

    # 4) Since we declared a "clear_" prefix, it expects to have a
    # "clear_attribute" method defined, which receives an attribute
    # name and implements the clearing logic.
    def clear_attribute(attribute)
      send("#{attribute}=", nil)
    end
  end
end
```

Run rake test, and all tests should be green again. ActiveModel::Attribute-Methods uses method_missing to compile both the clear_name and clear_email methods when they are first accessed. Their implementation simply invokes clear_attribute, passing the attribute name as a parameter.

If we want to define suffixes, instead of a prefix like clear_, we just need to use the attribute_method_suffix method and implement the method with the chosen suffix logic. As an example, let's implement name? and email? methods, which should return true if the respective attribute value is present, as in the following test:

`mail_form/3_attribute_suffix/test/mail_form_test.rb`

```ruby
test 'sample mail can ask if an attribute is present or not' do
  sample = SampleMail.new
  assert !sample.name?

  sample.name = "User"
  assert sample.name?

  sample.email = ""
  assert !sample.email?
end
```

When we run the test suite, our new test fails. To make it pass, let's define ? as a suffix, changing our MailForm::Base implementation to the following:

```
mail_form/3_attribute_suffix/lib/mail_form/base.rb
module MailForm
  class Base
    include ActiveModel::AttributeMethods

    attribute_method_prefix 'clear_'

    # 1) Add the attribute suffix
    attribute_method_suffix '?'

    def self.attributes(*names)
      attr_accessor *names
      define_attribute_methods names
    end

    protected

    def clear_attribute(attribute)
      send("#{attribute}=", nil)
    end

    # 2) Implement the logic required by the '?' suffix
    def attribute?(attribute)
      send(attribute).present?
    end
  end
end
```

Now we have both prefix and suffix methods defined and the tests passing. But what if we want to define both the prefix and the suffix at the same time? We could use the attribute_method_affix method, which accepts a hash specifying both the prefix and the suffix.

Active Record uses attributes methods extensively. An example is the attribute_before_type_cast method, which uses _before_type_cast as a suffix to return raw data, as stored in the database. The dirty functionality, which was moved to Active Model in Rails 3, is also built on top of ActiveModel::AttributeMethods and defines a handful of methods like attribute_changed?, reset_attribute!, and so on. You can check its source code in the Rails repository.[1]

---

1. https://github.com/rails/rails/tree/3-0-stable/activemodel/lib/active_model/dirty.rb

Aiming for an Active Model–Compliant API

Even though we added attributes to our models to store form data, we need to ensure that our model complies with the Active Model API; otherwise, we won't be able to use it in our controllers and views.

As usual, we are going to achieve this compliance through test-driven development, except this time we won't need to write the tests because Rails already provides all of them in a module called ActiveModel::Lint:: Tests. When included, this module defines several tests asserting that each method required in an Active Model–compliant API exists. Each of these tests, in order to run, expects an instance variable named @model to return the object we want to assert against. In our case, @model should contain an instance of SampleMail, which will be compliant if MailForm::Base is compliant. So, let's create a new test file called test/compliance_test.rb with the following:

mail_form/4_compliance/test/compliance_test.rb

```ruby
require 'test_helper'
require 'fixtures/sample_mail'

class ComplianceTest < ActiveSupport::TestCase
  include ActiveModel::Lint::Tests

  def setup
    @model = SampleMail.new
  end
end
```

When we run rake test, we get several failures, the first of which looks like this:

```
The object should respond_to to_model.
<false> is not true.
```

Rails controllers and views helpers, before invoking any method in our models, first call to_model and manipulate the returned result instead of the model directly. This allows ORM implementations that do not want to add Active Model methods to their API to return a proxy object where these methods are in fact defined. In our case, we want to add Active Model methods directly to MailForm::Base. Consequently, our to_ model implementation should simply return **self**, as shown here:

```ruby
def to_model
  self
end
```

Although we could add this method to MailForm::Base, we are not going to implement it ourselves. Instead, let's include ActiveModel::Conversion, which implements to_model exactly as we discussed and two other methods required by Active Model as well: to_key and to_param.

The to_key method should return an array of keys that uniquely identifies the model, if any exists, and it is used by dom_id in our views. The dom_id method was introduced in Rails 2.0 along with dom_class and a bunch of other helpers to better organize our views based on some conventions. For example, div_for(@post), where @post is an Active Record instance with an ID of 37, relies on both these methods to create a div where the ID attribute is equal to post-37 and the class attribute is post. For Active Record, dom_id simply returns an array with the record ID from the database.

On the other hand, to_param is used in routing and can be overwritten in any model to generate a unique URL for that model. When you invoke post_path(@post), Rails calls to_param in the @post object and uses its result to generate the final URL.

Because MailForm::Base objects are never persisted, they aren't uniquely identified, and both to_key and to_param should simply return nil, which is the default behavior provided by the ActiveModel::Conversion module. Let's include it inside the MailForm::Base class definition:

`mail_form/4_compliance/lib/mail_form/base.rb`

```ruby
module MailForm
  class Base
    include ActiveModel::Conversion
```

When we include this module and run rake test, we get different errors with the following messages:

```
The model should respond to model_name.
<false> is not true.
```

```
The model should respond to errors.
<false> is not true.
```

```
NameError: undefined local variable or method `attributes'
```

To fix the first failing test, we need to extend the MailForm::Base class with ActiveModel::Naming:

`mail_form/4_compliance/lib/mail_form/base.rb`

```ruby
module MailForm
  class Base
    include ActiveModel::Conversion
    extend ActiveModel::Naming
```

After extending our class with ActiveModel::Naming, it now responds to a method called model_name that returns an instance of ActiveModel::Name, which is a subclass of String. For all effects, ActiveModel::Name behaves as a string but provides a few extra methods such as human, singular, and others. Let's add a small test case to our suite showing these methods and what they return:

`mail_form/5_extensions/test/compliance_test.rb`

```
test "model_name exposes singular and human name" do
  assert_equal "sample_mail", model.class.model_name.singular
  assert_equal "Sample mail", model.class.model_name.human
end
```

This is similar to the behavior Active Record exhibits on Rails 3. The only difference is that Active Record supports internationalization (I18n) and Mail Form does not. Luckily, that can be easily fixed by extending MailForm::Base with ActiveModel::Translation. Let's write a test first:

`mail_form/5_extensions/test/compliance_test.rb`

```
test "model_name.human uses I18n" do
  begin
    I18n.backend.store_translations :en,
      :activemodel => { :models => { :sample_mail => "My Sample Mail" } }

    assert_equal "My Sample Mail", model.class.model_name.human
  ensure
    I18n.reload!
  end
end
```

The test adds a new translation to the I18n backend that contains the desired human name for the SampleMail class. We need to wrap the code in the begin ... ensure clause since we need to guarantee the I18n backend is reloaded, removing the translation we just stored. Let's update MailForm::Base to make the new test pass:

`mail_form/4_compliance/lib/mail_form/base.rb`

```
module MailForm
  class Base
    include ActiveModel::Conversion
    extend ActiveModel::Naming
    extend ActiveModel::Translation
```

After adding naming and translation behaviors to our model, rake test returns fewer failures, showing that we are moving forward. This time, the failures should contain one of these two messages:

```
The model should respond to errors.
<false> is not true.
```

```
NameError: undefined local variable or method `attributes'
```

The first failure is related to validations. Active Model does not say anything about validation macros (such as validates_presence_of), but it requires us to define a method named errors, which returns a Hash, and each value in this hash is an Array.

To handle the validations error, we just need to include ActiveModel:: Validations in our model:

mail_form/4_compliance/lib/mail_form/base.rb

```
module MailForm
  class Base
    include ActiveModel::Conversion
    extend ActiveModel::Naming
    extend ActiveModel::Translation
    include ActiveModel::Validations
```

Now our model responds to errors and valid?. Both methods are part of the API required for Active Model compliance and have default behavior exactly as in Active Record.

Besides those methods, ActiveModel::Validations also adds several validation macros such as validates_format_of, validates_inclusion_of, and even the new validates method. Since Rails 3 has several improvements on the validations side, we'll take a deeper look at these later in this chapter.

For now, let's run rake test and see what is left to make our test suite green again:

```
NameError: undefined local variable or method `attributes'
  lib/active_model/attribute_methods.rb:364:in `method_missing'
  lib/active_model/attribute_methods.rb:386:in `attribute_method?'
  lib/active_model/attribute_methods.rb:394:in `match_attribute_method?'
  lib/active_model/attribute_methods.rb:393:in `each'
  lib/active_model/attribute_methods.rb:393:in `match_attribute_method?'
  lib/active_model/attribute_methods.rb:378:in `respond_to?'
  lib/active_model/lint.rb:63:in `test_persisted?'
```

This is not a test failure but a Ruby error telling us that something unexpected happened. The only clue we can get from the backtrace is that it's related to the ActiveModel::AttributeMethods module. Fortunately, by taking a look at the module documentation,[2] we discover

---

2. https://github.com/rails/rails/tree/3-0-stable/activemodel/lib/active_model/attribute_methods.rb

that whenever we include ActiveModel::AttributeMethods in our models, it requires us to implement a method named attributes, which we haven't.

The error appears at this point only because ActiveModel::Lint::Tests makes use of respond_to?, which fails when you have the ActiveModel:: AttributeMethods module included but the attributes method is not implemented. If you use Active Record, you might have used the attributes method. It returns a hash with the attribute names as keys and their respective values. Implementing it in our model requires two steps: first we need to track all attributes defined by the developer, and then we need to use them to create an attributes hash. Let's write a test case:

`mail_form/5_extensions/test/mail_form_test.rb`

```ruby
test "can retrieve all attributes values" do
  sample = SampleMail.new
  sample.name = "John Doe"
  sample.email = "john.doe@example.com"
  assert_equal "John Doe", sample.attributes["name"]
  assert_equal "john.doe@example.com", sample.attributes["email"]
end
```

To make the test pass, our MailForm::Base should look like the following:

`mail_form/5_extensions/lib/mail_form/base.rb`

```ruby
module MailForm
  class Base
    include ActiveModel::Conversion
    extend ActiveModel::Naming
    extend ActiveModel::Translation
    include ActiveModel::Validations
    include ActiveModel::AttributeMethods

    # 1) Define a class inheritable attribute named _attributes
    # Let's use underscore to mark this method as internal to our gem
    class_attribute :_attributes
    self._attributes = []

    attribute_method_prefix 'clear_'
    attribute_method_suffix '?'

    def self.attributes(*names)
      attr_accessor *names
      define_attribute_methods names

      # 2) Add declared attributes to the list
      self._attributes += names
    end

    # 3) Create the attributes hash by iterating the list
```

```ruby
    def attributes
      self._attributes.inject({}) do |hash, attr|
        hash[attr.to_s] = send(attr)
        hash
      end
    end

    protected

    def clear_attribute(attribute)
      send("#{attribute}=", nil)
    end

    def attribute?(attribute)
      send(attribute).present?
    end
  end
end
```

To allow our MailForm::Base to be inheritable, our implementation uses the class_attribute method from Active Support to define the array that holds our attributes list. The class_attribute implementation ensures a child class has the same values as the parent but guarantees that setting a value in the child won't propagate to the parent.

When we run the test suite once again, our new test will pass, and the compliance suite now shows us a different error:

```
1) Failure:
test_persisted?(ComplianceTest)
  The model should respond to persisted?.
```

Now that we fixed the attributes error, we can finally see what's left to have our model fully compliant with the Active Model API: we just need to define the persisted? method.

The persisted? method is used by both our controllers and our views under different circumstances. For instance, whenever you do form_for(@model), it checks whether the model is persisted. If positive, it creates a form that does a PUT request; if not, it should do a POST request. The same happens in url_for when it generates a URL based on your model.

In Active Record, the object is persisted if it's saved in the database, in other words, if it's neither a new record nor destroyed. However, in our case, our object won't be saved in any database, and consequently persisted? should always return false.

Let's add the persisted? method to our MailForm::Base implementation:

`mail_form/6_delivery/lib/mail_form/base.rb`

```ruby
def persisted?
  false
end
```

This time, after running rake test, all tests pass! This means our model complies with the Active Model API. Well done!

Delivering the Form

The next step in our Mail Form implementation is to add the logic that delivers an email with the parameters sent through a form. Let's start by adding a failing test to test/mail_form_test.rb:

`mail_form/6_delivery/test/mail_form_test.rb`

```ruby
setup do
  ActionMailer::Base.deliveries.clear
end

test "delivers an email with attributes" do
  sample = SampleMail.new
  # Simulate data from the form
  sample.email = "user@example.com"
  sample.deliver

  assert_equal 1, ActionMailer::Base.deliveries.size
  mail = ActionMailer::Base.deliveries.last

  assert_equal ["user@example.com"], mail.from
  assert_match /Email: user@example\.com/, mail.body.encoded
end
```

From the test case, we can see that to send the email we need to invoke a method called deliver in our MailForm::Base object. The delivered email has as the sender the same value as the email attribute in our model. The body contains each attribute and their respective values.

Notice that in the mail.body assertion we need to call encoded (or to_s) to retrieve the proper value. This was not required in previous Rails versions, but now Rails 3 depends on the Mail[3] gem instead of TMail, which provides a more robust API when dealing with mails.

When we run the test we just added, we get a failure because the deliver method does not exist yet. Because our model has the concept of valid-

---

3. https://github.com/mikel/mail

ity from ActiveModel::Validations, the deliver method should just deliver the email if the Mail Form object is valid?. Let's define it:

`mail_form/6_delivery/lib/mail_form/base.rb`

```ruby
def deliver
  if valid?
    MailForm::Notifier.contact(self).deliver
  else
    false
  end
end
```

The class responsible for creating and delivering the email is MailForm:: Notifier. Let's implement it using the Action Mailer API:

`mail_form/6_delivery/lib/mail_form/notifier.rb`

```ruby
module MailForm
  class Notifier < ActionMailer::Base
    append_view_path File.expand_path("../../views", __FILE__)

    def contact(mail_form)
      @mail_form = mail_form
      mail(mail_form.headers)
    end
  end
end
```

The contact action in our mailer creates an assign called @mail_form and then invokes the headers method in the given Mail Form object. This method should return a hash with email data as keys like :to, :from, and :subject and should not be defined in MailForm::Base but in each child class. This is a simple but powerful API contract that allows a developer to customize the email delivery without a need to redefine or monkey-patch the Notifier class.

Our MailForm::Notifier also calls append_view_path, which adds lib/views inside our gem folder as a new location to search for templates. The last step before we run the test suite again is to autoload our new class:

`mail_form/6_delivery/lib/mail_form.rb`

```ruby
autoload :Notifier, 'mail_form/notifier'
```

Then, let's define the headers method in the SampleMail class:

`mail_form/6_delivery/test/fixtures/sample_mail.rb`

```ruby
def headers
  { :to => "recipient@example.com", :from => self.email }
end
```

Now when we run rake test, it fails with the following message:

```
1) Failure:
test_delivers_an_email_with_attributes(MailFormTest)
  <""> expected to be =~
</Email: user@example\.com/>.
```

This is expected since we haven't added a template to our mailer and the email body is blank. The mail template will show the message subject and print all attributes and their respective values:

`mail_form/6_delivery/lib/views/mail_form/notifier/contact.text.erb`

```erb
<%= message.subject %>

<% @mail_form.attributes.each do |key, value| -%>
  <%= @mail_form.class.human_attribute_name(key) %>: <%= value %>
<% end -%>
```

After running rake test, all tests should be green again, and our Mail Form implementation is finished.

Whenever we need to create a contact form, we just create a class that inherits from MailForm::Base, define our attributes and the email headers, and we are ready to go! To ensure it works exactly as we expect, let's test the whole process with an integration test.

Writing Integration Tests

To create an integration test for our Mail Form implementation, let's use the vendored Rails application in test/dummy and the Capybara helpers defined in ActiveSupport::IntegrationCase, like we did in the previous chapter:

`mail_form/6_delivery/test/integration/navigation_test.rb`

```ruby
require 'test_helper'

class NavigationTest < ActiveSupport::IntegrationCase
  setup do
    ActionMailer::Base.deliveries.clear
  end

  test "sends an e-mail after filling the contact form" do
    visit "/"

    fill_in "Name",    :with => "John Doe"
    fill_in "Email",   :with => "john.doe@example.com"
    fill_in "Message", :with => "MailForm rocks!"

    click_button "Deliver"
```

```
    assert_match "Your message was successfully sent.", page.body

    assert_equal 1, ActionMailer::Base.deliveries.size
    mail = ActionMailer::Base.deliveries.last

    assert_equal ["john.doe@example.com"], mail.from
    assert_equal ["recipient@example.com"], mail.to
    assert_match /Message: MailForm rocks!/, mail.body.encoded
  end
end
```

The integration test accesses the root path, which returns a form with name, email, and message fields. On submitting the form, the server delivers an email to a configured recipient with the written message and shows a success message to the user. To make the test pass, let's add the model, controller, views, and routes, starting with the latter:

mail_form/6_delivery/test/dummy/config/routes.rb

```ruby
Dummy::Application.routes.draw do
  resources :contact_forms, :only => :create
  root :to => "contact_forms#new"
end
```

The controller and view follow next:

mail_form/6_delivery/test/dummy/app/controllers/contact_forms_controller.rb

```ruby
class ContactFormsController < ApplicationController
  def new
    @contact_form = ContactForm.new
  end

  def create
    @contact_form = ContactForm.new(params[:contact_form])

    if @contact_form.deliver
      redirect_to root_url, :notice => "Your message was successfully sent."
    else
      render :action => "new"
    end
  end
end
```

mail_form/6_delivery/test/dummy/app/views/contact_forms/new.html.erb

```erb
<h1>New Contact Form</h1>

<%= form_for(@contact_form) do |f| %>
  <% if @contact_form.errors.any? %>
  <div id="errorExplanation">
    <h2>Oops, something went wrong:</h2>
    <ul>
```

```erb
    <% @contact_form.errors.full_messages.each do |msg| %>
      <li><%= msg %></li>
    <% end %>
    </ul>
  </div>
  <% end %>

  <div class="field">
    <%= f.label :name %><br />
    <%= f.text_field :name %>
  </div>
  <div class="field">
    <%= f.label :email %><br />
    <%= f.text_field :email %>
  </div>
  <div class="field">
    <%= f.label :message %><br />
    <%= f.text_field :message %>
  </div>
  <div class="actions">
    <%= f.submit "Deliver" %>
  </div>
<% end %>
```

And finally here's the model:

`mail_form/6_delivery/test/dummy/app/models/contact_form.rb`

```ruby
class ContactForm < MailForm::Base
  attributes :name, :email, :message

  def headers
    { :to => "recipient@example.com", :from => self.email }
  end
end
```

Because our tests use flash messages, we need to add them to the layout, just before the **yield** call:

`mail_form/6_delivery/test/dummy/app/views/layouts/application.html.erb`

```erb
<p style="color: green"><%= notice %></p>
```

With everything in place, let's run the test suite and...get an unexpected failure. Unless you are using Ruby 1.9.2, you will see the following error message:

```
1) Error:
test_sends_an_e-mail_after_filling_the_contact_form(NavigationTest):
ArgumentError: wrong number of arguments (1 for 0)
    app/controllers/contact_forms_controller.rb:7:in `initialize'
```

If you are using 1.9.2, you won't get an ArgumentError, but the test will fail nonetheless. The failure occurs because the initialize method in Mail-Form::Base, unlike Active Record, does not expect a hash as an argument. Notice that an Active Model–compliant API does not say anything about how our models should be initialized. Let's implement an initialize method, which receives a hash as an argument and sets attribute values:

mail_form/7_final/lib/mail_form/base.rb

```ruby
def initialize(attributes = {})
  attributes.each do |attr, value|
    self.send("#{attr}=", value)
  end unless attributes.blank?
end
```

After defining the previous method, our integration test works, showing that everything works as expected. Remember that if you go to the vendored application inside test/dummy, you can run rails s as in any other Rails application. Feel free to start your server, add some validations to your ContactForm class, and have some fun with it.

2.2 Taking It to the Next Level

In the previous section, we wrote our Mail Form gem with some basic features and added some integration testing to ensure it works. However, we can do a lot more with Active Model. Let's take a look at some examples.

Validators

In previous Rails versions, validation macros were monolithic blocks of code. However, Rails 3 introduces the concept of a *validator*, where each validation is a class. The previous validation macros, such as validates_presence_of, now delegate to their validator. Let's see the validates_presence_of macro as an example:

rails/activemodel/lib/active_model/validations/presence.rb

```ruby
def validates_presence_of(*attr_names)
  validates_with PresenceValidator, _merge_attributes(attr_names)
end
```

The validates_with method is responsible for initializing the given Active-Model::Validations::PresenceValidator class, while _merge_attributes converts the given attributes to a hash. When you invoke the following:

```ruby
validates_presence_of :name
```

you're actually doing this:

```
validates_with PresenceValidator, :attributes => [:name]
```

which is roughly the same as the following:

```
validate PresenceValidator.new(:attributes => [:name])
```

Along with validators, Rails 3 also added the validates method, which allows you to set several validations on one attribute in just one method call:

```
validates :name, :presence => true
```

This, again, at the end is just the same as the following:

```
validate PresenceValidator.new(:attributes => [:name])
```

The question is, how does Rails know that the :presence key should use the PresenceValidator? Simple: it first converts the :presence key to "PresenceValidator" and then tries to find a constant named PresenceValidator in the current class, just like the following:

```
"#{key.to_s.camelize}Validator".constantize
```

This is important to discuss because now we can add any validator to any class, relying solely on Ruby's constant lookup. To understand exactly how it works, let's start a new irb session and type the following:

```
module Foo
  module Bar
  end
end

class Baz
  include Foo
end

Baz::Bar # => Foo::Bar
```

Notice how the last line of the script in the previous code returns Foo::Bar even if Bar is not defined inside the Baz class. This happens because whenever a constant is looked up, Ruby searches inside all objects in the ancestor chain. Since Foo is included in Baz, Foo is an ancestor of Baz, allowing Ruby to find the Foo::Bar constant (you can check Baz ancestors by typing Baz.ancestors in the previous irb session).

This means we can add an :absence option to the validates method of any class by simply implementing the AbsenceValidator inside a module and including this module in the desired classes.

To showcase how we can use this in practice, we are going to implement an absence validator in our MailForm::Base. Since a lot of spam usually comes through contact forms, we are going to use the absence validator as a honey pot.

The honey pot works by creating a field, such as nickname, and hiding it with CSS. This way, humans do not see the field and consequently do not fill it in, while robots will fill it in like any other field. So whenever the nickname value is present, the email should not be sent because it is definitely spam.

Let's start by writing a simple test for it:

`mail_form/7_final/test/mail_form_test.rb`

```ruby
test "validates absence of nickname" do
  sample = SampleMail.new(:nickname => "Spam")
  assert !sample.valid?
  assert_equal ["is invalid"], sample.errors[:nickname]
end
```

The test shows the record must be invalid if the nickname field contains any value. So, let's add the nickname field with :absence validation to our SampleMail object:

`mail_form/7_final/test/fixtures/sample_mail.rb`

```ruby
attributes :nickname
validates :nickname, :absence => true
```

When we run rake test, we will get a failure, because SampleMail can no longer be loaded because AbsenceValidator is not defined anywhere. Let's create it:

`mail_form/7_final/lib/mail_form/validators.rb`

```ruby
module MailForm
  module Validators
    class AbsenceValidator < ActiveModel::EachValidator
      def validate_each(record, attribute, value)
        record.errors.add(attribute, :invalid, options) unless value.blank?
      end
    end
  end
end
```

Our validator inherits from EachValidator. For each attribute given on initialization, EachValidator calls the validate_each method with the record, the attribute, and its respective value. For each attribute, we add an error message, unless the value is blank.

Next, let's include MailForm::Validators in MailForm::Base:

`mail_form/7_final/lib/mail_form/base.rb`

```
include MailForm::Validators
```

This will add MailForm::Validators to the MailForm::Base ancestors chain. So, whenever we give :absence as a key to validates, it will search for an AbsenceValidator constant, find it inside MailForm::Validators, and initialize it, similar to what it did with the PresenceValidator.

To ensure it really works, we just need to autoload our validators container:

`mail_form/7_final/lib/mail_form.rb`

```
autoload :Validators, 'mail_form/validators'
```

Run rake test, and all tests should pass again. The beauty of this implementation is that adding the :absence key to validates did not require us to register the option anywhere. Those options are discovered at runtime using Ruby's constant lookup.

Add this new nickname field to your contact form views and hide it with some CSS, and we are ready to stop some bots. It's up to you to write an integration test for it, since we still have some more Active Model investigation to do.

Callbacks

Wouldn't it be cool if we could provide hooks around the deliver method so we could add some behavior *before* and *after* the delivery? This is quite easy to achieve with ActiveModel::Callbacks. First, let's create a test case with the desired functionality:

`mail_form/7_final/test/mail_form_test.rb`

```
test "provides before and after deliver hooks" do
  sample = SampleMail.new
  sample.deliver
  assert_equal [:before, :after], sample.callbacks
end
```

The test calls the deliver method and asserts that one before and one after callback were executed. Let's declare those callbacks in our SampleMail:

`mail_form/7_final/test/fixtures/sample_mail.rb`

```
before_deliver do
  callbacks << :before
end
```

```
after_deliver do
  callbacks << :after
end

def callbacks
  @callbacks ||= []
end
```

Finally, let's add support to callbacks in MailForm::Base. This can be done in three steps: extend our class with ActiveModel::Callbacks functionality, then define our callbacks, and finally overwrite deliver implementation to run the callbacks before and after delivering:

`mail_form/7_final/lib/mail_form/base.rb`

```
# 1) Add callbacks behavior
extend ActiveModel::Callbacks

# 2) Define the callbacks. The line below will create both before_deliver
# and after_deliver callbacks with the same semantics as in Active Record
define_model_callbacks :deliver

# 3) Change deliver to run the callbacks
def deliver
  if valid?
    _run_deliver_callbacks do
      MailForm::Notifier.contact(self).deliver
    end
  else
    false
  end
end
```

As Active Record callbacks, you can give procs, strings, symbols, and any object that responds to the callback name. Feel free to try these options!

2.3 Wrapping Up

In this chapter, we learned how to use Active Model to quickly create our own models that play seamlessly with Rails controllers and views. We talked about ActiveModel::AttributeMethods, ActiveModel::Conversion, ActiveModel::Naming, ActiveModel::Translation, ActiveModel::Validations, and finally ActiveModel::Callbacks. We also dove into Rails 3 validators and how we can easily extend the validates method behavior.

Even after all that, Active Model still has more to offer. Take a look at ActiveModel::Dirty, ActiveModel::MassAssignmentSecurity, ActiveModel:: Observing, and ActiveModel::Serialization as well. They allow us to bring dirty attributes, accessible attributes, observers, and serializers (such as to_xml and to_json), as in Active Record, right into our models.

Finally, if you enjoyed Mail Form here, check out the Mail Form by Plataforma Tec,[4] which is a production-ready gem, created with the same concepts explored in this chapter. It also has additional features, such as attachment handling and the ability to append request information.

In the next chapter, let's go back to studying the Rails rendering stack and extend it to look for a template in the database instead of the filesystem, keeping an eye on performance.

---

4. https://github.com/plataformatec/mail_form

In this chapter, we'll see

- How to customize Rails rendering stack to look up templates from the database
- How Ruby Hash lookup works
- How to speed up controllers with ActionController::Metal

## Chapter 3

Retrieving View Templates from Custom Stores

In Section 1.3, *Understanding Rails Rendering Stack*, on page 11, we analyzed Rails' rendering stack and learned that its main responsibility is to normalize options and send them to ActionView::Base. Each controller holds an instance of ActionView::Base called view_context that receives those normalized options through the render method and uses them to find, compile, and render a specific template.

At first, you may find *view context* to be an awkward name, but there is a good explanation behind it. In a Rails 3 application, when we render a template, that template is read from the filesystem, and its code is compiled to Ruby code. This Ruby code is executed within the context of an object, and in Rails 3, this is the view_context object. All helpers available in our templates, such as form_for and link_to, are actually defined in modules included in the view_context object.

Upon initialization, the view_context also receives from the controller an object called view_paths as an argument. The view_paths is a collection of objects responsible for finding templates given a set of conditions. All controllers in a Rails application have one view path by default, which is a filesystem path pointing to app/views. Given a set of conditions like template name, locale, and format, this view path finds a specific template under app/views. For instance, whenever we have an HTML request at the index action of a UsersController, this default view path will attempt to pick a template at app/views/users/index.html.*. If the desired template is found, it's then compiled and rendered, as shown in Figure 3.1, on the next page.

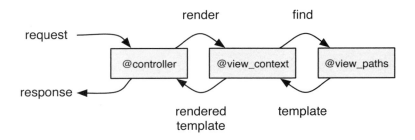

Figure 3.1: RENDERING WORKFLOW BETWEEN CONTROLLER, VIEW CONTEXT, AND VIEW PATH

In Section 2.1, *Delivering the Form*, on page 30, we manipulated the view path in our MailForm::Notifier object to include another path in the template lookup:

```
module MailForm
  class Notifier < ActionMailer::Base
    append_view_path File.expand_path("../../views", __FILE__)
  end
end
```

The previous code is basically expressing that if a template cannot be found under app/views, it should look within the lib/views directory inside our gem next.

Rails has allowed us to customize template compiling and rendering since its first releases (we will see how in the next chapter). However, the ability to customize and handle several view paths was introduced only in Rails 2.0. Rails 3 improves upon that by allowing us to encapsulate in any object the logic that finds a template.

This improvement means we are no longer forced to store view templates in the filesystem. We can now store them anywhere we want as long as we provide an object that knows how to find them. We call this object the *template resolver*, and it must comply with the Resolver API.

Rails 3 provides an abstract resolver implementation, called Action-View::Resolver. In this chapter we're going to use it to create a resolver that uses the database as a template store, so we can store our pages in the database and edit them through a web interface using our favorite template handler (such as Liquid, ERb, or Haml). The nice thing about this is that we need only one scaffold and a few lines of code!

3.1   Setting Up a SqlResolver

This time, instead of using enginex to create and implement the desired functionality as a gem, we will develop the template management system by building a Rails application called templater. So, let's create it using the command line:

```
rails new templater
```

Next, let's define the model that will hold templates in the database using the Rails scaffold generator:

```
bundle exec rails generate scaffold SqlTemplate body:text path:string \
  format:string locale:string handler:string partial:boolean
```

The body attribute is a text column used to store the whole template, the path should store a string similar to a filesystem path (for instance the index action under UsersController will have users/index as the path), format and locale hold the template format and its locale, the handler stores the template handler (for example, Liquid, ERb, and Haml), and finally partial tells us whether the stored template is a partial.

Before executing the created migration, let's just make one change in it, setting **false** as the default value for the partial attribute:

```
t.boolean :partial, :default => false
```

And now we are ready to run our migrations:

```
rake db:migrate
```

So far, no surprises. Next, let's create a *template resolver*, which will use the SqlTemplate model to read templates from the database and expose them according to the Resolver API described next.

The Resolver API

The Resolver API is composed of a single method, called find_all, which should return an array of templates and has the following signature:

```
def find_all(name, prefix, partial, details, cache_key)
```

For an HTML request at the index action of a UsersController, those arguments are exactly as shown here:

```
find_all("index", "users", false, { :formats => [:html],
  :locale => [:en, :en], :handlers => [:erb, :builder, :rjs] }, nil)
```

For this simple request, we can see that name maps to the action name, while prefix refers to the controller name. Next, partial is a boolean that tells whether the template being rendered is a partial, and details is a hash with extra information for the lookup, such as the request formats, the current I18n locale followed by the default locale, and the available template handlers. For now, we'll consider that this request happened in the development environment, where caching is disabled, and so the cache_key is nil. We will discuss caching later.

Rails 3 provides an abstract resolver implementation, called Action-View::Resolver, which we are going to use as the base for our resolver. Its source code is shown next, but for now, let's simply focus only on the find_all and find_template methods:

```
rails/actionpack/lib/action_view/template/resolver.rb
module ActionView
  class Resolver
    def initialize
      @cached = Hash.new { |h1,k1| h1[k1] =
        Hash.new { |h2,k2| h2[k2] = Hash.new { |h3, k3| h3[k3] = {} } } }
    end

    def clear_cache
      @cached.clear
    end

    # Normalizes the arguments and passes it on to find_template.
    def find_all(name, prefix=nil, partial=false, details={}, key=nil)
      cached(key, prefix, name, partial) do
        find_templates(name, prefix, partial, details)
      end
    end

  private

    def caching?
      @caching ||= Rails.application.config.cache_classes
    end

    def find_templates(name, prefix, partial, details)
      raise NotImplementedError
    end

    def cached(key, prefix, name, partial)
      return yield unless key && caching?
      @cached[key][prefix][name][partial] ||= yield
    end
  end
end
```

The find_all method implements a basic caching mechanism where the block given to cached is yielded if no previous entry exists in the cache.

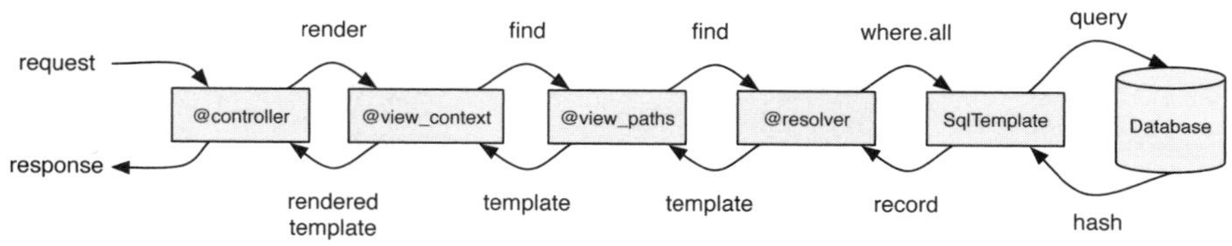

Figure 3.2: Template lookup with SqlTemplate

And, if in fact no entry exists in the cache, find_templates is invoked. The find_templates method raises a NotImplementedError, indicating it should actually be implemented in child classes.

Next, inherit from ActionView::Resolver and implement the find_template method using the SqlTemplate API to retrieve templates from the database, resulting in the same template lookup, as shown in Figure 3.2.

Writing the Code

Let's call our resolver implementation SqlTemplate::Resolver and implement it in three main steps. The first receives the name, prefix, partial, and details as arguments and normalizes them. From the normalized arguments, we create a SQL statement and query the database. This query returns an array of records from the database that is then used to create an array of ActionView::Template instances.

Let's write a test first to demonstrate the functionality we want.

templater/1_resolvers/test/unit/sql_template_test.rb

```ruby
require 'test_helper'

class SqlTemplateTest < ActiveSupport::TestCase
  test "resolver returns a template with the saved body" do
    resolver = SqlTemplate::Resolver.new
    details  = { :formats => [:html], :locale => [:en], :handlers => [:erb] }

    # 1) Assert our resolver cannot find any template as the database is empty
    # find_all(name, prefix, partial, details)
    assert resolver.find_all("index", "posts", false, details).empty?

    # 2) Create a template in the database
    SqlTemplate.create!(
      :body => "<%= 'Hi from SqlTemplate!' %>",
      :path => "posts/index",
```

```
        :format => "html",
        :locale => "en",
        :handler => "erb",
        :partial => false)

    # 3) Assert that a template can now be found
    template = resolver.find_all("index", "posts", false, details).first
    assert_kind_of ActionView::Template, template

    # 4) Assert specific information about the found template
    assert_equal "<%= 'Hi from SqlTemplate!' %>", template.source
    assert_match /SqlTemplate - \d+ - "posts\/index"/, template.identifier
    assert_equal ActionView::Template::Handlers::ERB, template.handler
    assert_equal [:html], template.formats
    assert_equal "posts/index", template.virtual_path
  end
end
```

The find method in our resolver should return an ActionView::Template instance. This template instance is initialized as follows:

```
ActionView::Template.new(source, identifier, handler, details)
```

The source is the body of the template stored in the database. The identifier is an unique string used to represent the template. We will ensure this uniqueness by adding the template ID in the database to it.

The handler is the object responsible for rendering the template. This object is not a string—like we stored in the database—but an object that is retrieved using the method registered_template_handler from Action-View::Template:

```
ActionView::Template.registered_template_handler("erb")
  # => ActionView::Template::Handlers::ERB
```

Finally, the last parameter given on template initialization is a hash that should contain three details: the :format of the template found, the last time the template was updated as :updated_at, and a :virtual_path that represents the template.

Since templates are no longer required to be in the filesystem, they do not necessarily have a path, and this breaks a couple of Rails features that depend explicitly on it. One example is the I18n shortcut t(".message") inside your views. It uses the template filesystem path to retrieve the translation, so whenever you are inside a template at app/views/users/index, the shortcut attempts to find the I18n translation at "users.index.message".

To circumvent this need for a path, Rails 3 introduced the :virtual_path. You can store your templates anywhere and give them any source or any identifier, but you need to provide a :virtual_path that represents what the path would be if this template was stored in the filesystem. This allows t(".message") to work as expected by setting the virtual path to be users/index.

With tests in place and an understanding of how templates are initialized, let's implement our resolver by inheriting from ActionView::Resolver and implementing find_template.

It's important to consider in our resolver that the order of the given details matters. In other words, if the locale array contains [:es, :en], a template in Spanish (:es) has higher preference than the one in English, in case both exist. To solve this in our resolver, one option is to generate an order clause for each detail and get the result properly sorted from the database. Another option is to sort the returned templates in Rails. However, for simplicity, instead of passing all locales and formats to the SQL query, let's simply pick the first ones from the array.

Without further ado, let's implement our resolver:

```
templater/1_resolvers/app/models/sql_template.rb
class SqlTemplate < ActiveRecord::Base
  validates :body, :path, :presence => true

  validates :format,  :inclusion => Mime::SET.symbols.map(&:to_s)
  validates :locale,  :inclusion => I18n.available_locales.map(&:to_s)
  validates :handler, :inclusion =>
    ActionView::Template::Handlers.extensions.map(&:to_s)

  class Resolver < ActionView::Resolver
    protected

    def find_templates(name, prefix, partial, details)
      conditions = {
        :path    => normalize_path(name, prefix),
        :locale  => normalize_array(details[:locale]).first,
        :format  => normalize_array(details[:formats]).first,
        :handler => normalize_array(details[:handlers]),
        :partial => partial || false
      }

      ::SqlTemplate.where(conditions).map do |record|
        initialize_template(record)
      end
    end
  end
```

```ruby
# Normalize name and prefix, so the tuple ["index", "users"] becomes
# "users/index" and the tuple ["template", nil] becomes "template".
def normalize_path(name, prefix)
  prefix.present? ? "#{prefix}/#{name}" : name
end

# Normalize arrays by converting all symbols to strings.
def normalize_array(array)
  array.map(&:to_s)
end

# Initialize an ActionView::Template object based on the record found.
def initialize_template(record)
  source = record.body
  identifier = "SqlTemplate - #{record.id} - #{record.path.inspect}"
  handler = ActionView::Template.registered_template_handler(record.handler)

  details = {
    :format => Mime[record.format],
    :updated_at => record.updated_at,
    :virtual_path => virtual_path(record.path, record.partial)
  }

  ActionView::Template.new(source, identifier, handler, details)
end

# Make paths as "users/user" become "users/_user" for partials.
def virtual_path(path, partial)
  return path unless partial
  if index = path.rindex("/")
    path.insert(index + 1, "_")
  else
    "_#{path}"
  end
end
  end
end
```

Our implementation normalizes the given arguments, queries the database, and creates template objects from the result set. We also add several validations to our model. We ensure that the body and path values cannot be blank, and we also guarantee that a valid format, locale, and handler are supplied.

As a result of adding some validations to our models, some functionals tests are failing since our fixtures now contain invalid data. To make them pass, let's change the fixture at test/fixtures/sql_templates.yml to include a valid format, locale, and handler:

`templater/1_resolvers/test/fixtures/sql_templates.yml`

```yaml
one:
  path: "some/path"
  format: "html"
  locale: "en"
  handler: "erb"
  partial: false
  body: "Body"
```

It Works!

Now with our resolver implemented and a green test suite, we get to create a new scaffold and make it use templates from the database, instead of the filesystem. So, let's create a user scaffold by running the following command:

```
bundle exec rails generate scaffold User name:string
```

And run our migrations next:

```
rake db:migrate
```

We can now start the server, access /users, and perform all CRUD operations as usual.

Next, let's access the /sql_templates path and create a new template by filling the template body with the same contents as the file in app/views/users/index.html.erb; setting the path with users/index; setting the format, locale, and handler to html, en, and erb, respectively; and keeping the partial box unchecked.

Save this new template, and head back to the /users path. Now, delete the view file app/views/users/index.html.erb, and rerender the page. You should get a "Template is missing" error, but don't worry, because we expected that. The template is stored in the database, but we still haven't told the UsersController to use our new resolver to retrieve it. Let's do it by adding the following line to UsersController:

`templater/2_running_tests/app/controllers/users_controller.rb`

```ruby
class UsersController < ApplicationController
  append_view_path SqlTemplate::Resolver.new
```

When we refresh the page at /users, we see the whole index page once again, retrieved from the database! And, while the template is in the database, the layout still comes from the filesystem. In other words, in a single request, we can get templates from different resolvers in our view paths.

Feel free to head back to /sql_templates, manipulate the body of the stored template, and notice that our index action in the UsersController will change accordingly. The fact we can achieve this behavior in so few lines of code showcases the power of the ActionView::Resolver abstraction introduced in Rails 3.

Before we move to the next section, let's run the test suite once again. It turns out that a test is failing with an error message:

```
1) Error:
test_should_get_index(UsersControllerTest)
ActionView::MissingTemplate: Missing template users/index with
  :locale=>[:en, :en]
  :formats=>[:html]
  app/controllers/users_controller.rb
  in `index'
```

This happens because we deleted the template from the filesystem. Although we added the same template to our development database, our test database remains clean, raising this MissingTemplate error in the test environment. To fix this, let's change our sql_templates fixture.

templater/2_running_tests/test/fixtures/sql_templates.yml

```
one:
  path: "users/index"
  format: "html"
  locale: "en"
  handler: "erb"
  partial: false
  body: "<h1>Listing users</h1>
<table>
  <tr>
    <th>Name</th>
    <th></th>
    <th></th>
    <th></th>
  </tr>
<%% @users.each do |user| %>
  <tr>
    <td><%%= user.name %></td>
    <td><%%= link_to 'Show', user %></td>
    <td><%%= link_to 'Edit', edit_user_path(user) %></td>
    <td><%%= link_to 'Destroy', user,
      :confirm => 'Are you sure?', :method => :delete %></td>
  </tr>
<%% end %>
</table>
<br />
<%%= link_to 'New user', new_user_path %>"
```

Our fixture is just a copy of the template. The only caveat is that Rails parses fixtures with ERb, so we need to escape our ERb tags in the previous fixture using <%% ... %>. And that's all—tests are all green again.

3.2 Configuring Our Resolver for Production

Our SqlTemplate::Resolver already works, but before we use it in production, we have to deal with two scenarios: template caching and expiring this cache whenever a template is modified.

As mentioned earlier, Rails gives our resolver a cache_key through the find_all method. In the following sections, let's learn why Rails creates this cache key and how our resolver uses it.

The Resolvers Cache

As you learned in the code on page 59, ActionView::Resolver's find_all method automatically caches templates using the cached method. These templates are stored in a nested hash created on initialization and referenced by the instance variable @cached. The resolver also exposes a clear_cache method to clear the cache hash, and it caches templates only if Rails.application.config.cache_classes returns true.

Before proceeding, it's important to discuss some implementation details. For instance, why do we use a nested hash to cache templates instead of using just an array or hash as the key? In Ruby, we could store the templates in the @cached hash in the different ways.

```
# Nested hash
@cached[key][prefix][name][partial]

# Simple hash with array as key
@cached[[key, prefix, name, partial]]

# Simple hash with hash as key
@cached[:key => key, :prefix => prefix, :name => name, :partial => partial]
```

All three cache implementations shown give us the desired behavior. However, there is a difference between them: performance. We need to explore how Ruby does hash lookups to understand this.

Ruby Hash Lookup

Whenever we store a value for a given key in a Hash object, Ruby stores three things: the given key, the given value, and the object hash for the given key. This hash is the result of the Object#hash method called on

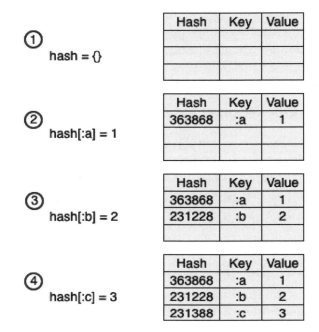

Figure 3.3: ILLUSTRATION OF WHAT A HASH STORES FOR EACH ENTRY. KEEP IN MIND THE RUBY IMPLEMENTATION DOES NOT USE A TABLE STRUCTURE BUT USES POINTERS INSTEAD, ALTHOUGH THE TABLE IS AN EASY WAY TO REPRESENT HOW IT WORKS.

the object given as the key. There is an easy way to prove that Ruby Hash in fact relies on Object#hash; just start an irb session, and type the following:

```ruby
class NoHash
  undef_method :hash
end

hash = Hash.new
hash[NoHash.new] = 1
# => NoMethodError: undefined method `hash' for #<NoHash:0x101643820>
```

If we undefine the hash method in our object, it can no longer be stored in the hash. Adding an element to the hash is similar to creating a new entry in a table, as shown in Figure 3.3.

Whenever we attempt to retrieve the value for a given key in a Hash object, like hash[:b], Ruby first calculates the Object#hash for this given key and then searches whether one or more entries in the Hash object have this same hash value. For instance, the value returned by :b.hash is 231228 in Figure 3.3, on the facing page. Seeing that there are one or more entries with the value 231228, Ruby then compares whether any of the keys for these entries is equal to the given key, using the equality operator eql?. Since :b.eql?(:b) returns **true**, accessing hash[:b] in our example successfully returns 2 as the result.

To prove that Ruby in fact uses Object#hash to localize entries, let's start another irb session and do a few experiments.

```
hash    = {}
object = Object.new

hash[object] = 1
hash[object] # => 1

def object.hash; 123; end

hash[object] # => nil
hash         # => {#<Object:0x1016e3de8>=>1}
```

This time, we used an arbitrary Ruby object as a hash key, and we could successfully set and get values. However, after we modified the value returned by object#hash, the value could not be found, even though the same object is still in the hash.

The reason Ruby stores Object#hash for each key is to provide faster lookups. Comparing hash values (integers) is much faster than comparing each object stored in the hash.

This implementation implies that the performance hit in finding a value in the hash is not just in the eql? method but also in calculating Object#hash for the given key. Remember, we could choose to implement our resolver cache using a nested hash or a simple hash with arrays as the key or a simple hash with hashes as keys. We should choose the first, because in the nested hash case, the hash keys are strings or booleans, and Ruby knows how to calculate the Object#hash value for these very fast. On the other hand, calculating Object#hash and equality for arrays and hashes is more expensive.

We can demonstrate this in another irb session:

```ruby
require "benchmark"
foo   = "foo"
bar   = "bar"
array = [foo, bar]
hash  = {:a => foo, :b => bar}

nested_hash = Hash.new { |h,k| h[k] = {} }
nested_hash[foo][bar] = true

array_hash = { array => true }
hash_hash  = { hash => true }

Benchmark.realtime { 1000.times { nested_hash[foo][bar] } }  # => 0.000474
Benchmark.realtime { 1000.times { array_hash[array] } }      # => 0.000900
Benchmark.realtime { 1000.times { hash_hash[hash] } }        # => 0.001364
```

We can see the nested hash implementation yields better results. Although the choice for a nested hash *apparently* does not yield real gains, the concepts we learned about Hash lookups in Ruby are fundamental to understand the next section.

The Cache Key

We already know that our resolvers come with a built-in cache. We also know that this cache uses a nested hash to store the templates found. If we take another look at the find_all implementation, we can see this cache depends on four variables:

```ruby
def find_all(name, prefix=nil, partial=false, details={}, cache_key=nil)
  cached(cache_key, prefix, name, partial) do
    find_templates(name, prefix, partial, details)
  end
end
```

In addition to prefix, name, and partial variables, the cache depends also on the cache_key, which is generated by Rails using all the values in the details hash.

Remember how we show that calculating the Object#hash and equality for hash objects is a bit expensive when compared to simpler structures like strings? If we use details as the key in the cache's nested hash, it would be slow since details is a hash of arrays:

```ruby
# Slow because details is a hash of arrays
@cached[details][prefix][name][partial]
```

Instead, Rails generates a simple Ruby object for each details hash and sends it as cache_key to resolvers. The whole process is similar to the following lines:

```
# Generate an object for the details hash
@details_key ||= {}
key = @details_key[details] ||= Object.new

# And send it to each resolver
resolver.find_all(name, prefix, partial, details, key)

# Inside the resolver, the cache is fast because key is simply an Object
@cached[key][prefix][name][partial]
```

The details hash is still used as hash key, but the difference is that it happens just once in a request and not every time a template or layout is looked up by each resolver.

Let's fire up irb once again and do our last benchmark in this chapter. Our benchmark will show how accessing a hash using a simple Object, like the cache_key does, compares with using a hash of arrays, like the details hash does:

```
require "benchmark"
cache_key = Object.new
details   = {
  :formats  => [:html, :xml, :json],
  :locale   => [:en],
  :handlers => [:erb, :builder, :rjs]
}

hash_1 = { cache_key => 10 }
hash_2 = { details => 10 }

Benchmark.realtime { 1000.times { hash_1[cache_key] } } # => 0.000372
Benchmark.realtime { 1000.times { hash_2[details] } }   # => 0.003700
```

Ten times slower is quite a difference! For applications that require high performance, these milliseconds can easily mount up in requests that render several collections and partials, dramatically affecting the response time. In some benchmarks done with Rails, using the details hash *took up to 10 percent of the time spent in the rendering stack*, while using the cache_key reduces this to less than 1 percent.

Expiring the Cache

Since the cache inside resolvers is handled automatically by Rails, we only need to worry about expiring the cache using the Resolver#clear_cache method. However, since the cache is in the resolver instance, in order to expire these caches, we would need to track all instances of SqlTemplate::Resolver and call clear_cache in each of them whenever we add or update a template in the database.

However, does it really make sense to create several SqlTemplate::Resolver instances? If we consider that the cache is in the instance, creating several instances would actually create several caches, reducing their effectiveness. Therefore, we don't want several resolvers instances. We want only one shared across the entire application.

In other words, what we need is a *singleton* class. Luckily, Ruby has a Singleton module in its Standard Library, which does all the hard work for us. By including this module in SqlTemplate::Resolver, it makes Sql-Template::Resolver.new a private method and exposes SqlTemplate::Resolver. instance instead, which always returns the same object.

Also, by having a singleton object, it's very easy to expire the cache. Since we can always access the instantiated resolver with SqlTemplate:: Resolver.instance, we just need to call clear_cache on it every time we save a SqlTemplate instance.

So, let's get started with those changes. The first one is to require and include Singleton inside SqlTemplate::Resolver:

`templater/3_improving/app/models/sql_template.rb`

```ruby
require "singleton"
include Singleton
```

After doing this simple change, we should update both app/controllers/ users_controller.rb and test/unit/sql_template_test.rb to call SqlTemplate:: Resolver.instance instead of SqlTemplate::Resolver.new:

`templater/3_improving/app/controllers/users_controller.rb`

```ruby
append_view_path SqlTemplate::Resolver.instance
```

`templater/3_improving/test/unit/sql_template_test.rb`

```ruby
resolver = SqlTemplate::Resolver.instance
```

With our singleton resolver in place, let's write a test in test/unit/sql_tem-plate_test.rb, which asserts that our cache is properly expired. This new test should update the SqlTemplate from fixtures and assert our resolver will return the updated template:

`templater/3_improving/test/unit/sql_template_test.rb`

```ruby
test "sql_template expires the cache on update" do
  cache_key = Object.new
  resolver  = SqlTemplate::Resolver.instance
  details   = { :formats => [:html], :locale => [:en], :handlers => [:erb] }

  t = resolver.find_all("index", "users", false, details, cache_key).first
  assert_match /Listing users/, t.source
```

```
    sql_template = sql_templates(:one)
    sql_template.update_attributes(:body => "New body for template")

    t = resolver.find_all("index", "users", false, details, cache_key).first
    assert_equal "New body for template", t.source
end
```

Notice we generated a fake cache_key with Object.new to pass to find_all because the cache is activated only if a cache key is supplied.

Finally, to make our test pass, let's add an after_save callback to SqlTemplate, right after the model validations:

`templater/3_improving/app/models/sql_template.rb`

```
after_save do
  SqlTemplate::Resolver.instance.clear_cache
end
```

And that's it. We finished our SqlTemplate::Resolver, and it's ready for prime time!

3.3   Serving Templates with Metal

Now that we have our own production-ready SqlTemplate::Resolver with cache-expiring mechanism, we are ready to take it to the next level. In the following sections, let's use this template management system as a simple CMS.

CmsController

We already can create, update, and delete templates by accessing /sql_templates; now we just need to expose them depending on the accessed URL. To achieve this, let's map all requests under /cms/* to a controller that will use our resolver to find the template in the database and then render them back to the client. A request at /cms/about should render a SqlTemplate stored in the database with path equals to about.

We are able to implement this functionality with a few lines of code. Let's start with an integration test:

`templater/3_improving/test/integration/cms_test.rb`

```
require 'test_helper'

class CmsTest < ActiveSupport::TestCase
  include Capybara
```

```
test "can access any page in SqlTemplate" do
  visit "/sql_templates"
  click_link "New Sql template"

  fill_in "Body",    :with => "My first CMS template"
  fill_in "Path",    :with => "about"
  fill_in "Format",  :with => "html"
  fill_in "Locale",  :with => "en"
  fill_in "Handler", :with => "erb"

  click_button "Create Sql template"
  assert_match "Sql template was successfully created.", page.body

  visit "/cms/about"
  assert_match "My first CMS template", page.body
  end
end
```

Since our test uses Capybara helpers, let's add Capybara to our application Gemfile:

`templater/3_improving/Gemfile`

```
group :test do
  gem "capybara", "0.4.0"
end
```

And then let's configure it in test/test_helper.rb:

`templater/3_improving/test/test_helper.rb`

```
require "capybara/rails"
Rails.backtrace_cleaner.remove_silencers!
Capybara.default_driver = :rack_test
```

To make our new test pass, let's write a route that will map to our CmsController:

`templater/3_improving/config/routes.rb`

```
match "cms/*page", :to => "cms#respond"
```

This route maps all requests at /cms/* to the respond action in the CmsController, which we implement like this:

`templater/3_improving/app/controllers/cms_controller.rb`

```
class CmsController < ApplicationController
  append_view_path SqlTemplate::Resolver.instance

  def respond
    render :template => params[:page]
  end
end
```

We simply pass the given route as a template name, which will be looked up in our SqlTemplate::Resolver. Our test suite is green once again!

If you want to test it manually, fire up the server, go to /sql_templates, create a new template with path equals to about, and add some content. Then just hit /cms/about and see your new page exhibited!

Playing with Metal

Our CmsController inherits from ApplicationController, which inherits from ActionController::Base, and consequently it comes with all the functionality. It includes all helpers, adds CSRF protection, allows you to hide actions with hide_action, supports flash messages, adds the respond_to syntax, and does a lot more that we won't need in our controller since it handles only GET requests. Wouldn't it be nice if we could somehow have a simpler controller with just the behavior we need?

We have already discussed Abstract Controller and how it provides a basic structure that is shared between Action Mailer and Action Controller. However, AbstractController::Base does not know anything about HTTP. Building all the required support from scratch would require some effort. On the other hand, ActionController::Base comes with the whole package. Isn't there a point in the middle?

Actually, there is! It's called ActionController::Metal. ActionController::Metal inherits from AbstractController::Base and implements the minimum functionality required for our controllers to be a valid Rack application and work with HTTP.

By taking a quick look at ActionController::Base in the Rails source code, we notice it inherits from Metal and adds a bunch of behavior:

`rails/actionpack/lib/action_controller/base.rb`

```ruby
module ActionController
  class Base < Metal
    abstract!

    include AbstractController::Layouts
    include AbstractController::Translation

    include ActionController::Helpers

    include ActionController::HideActions
    include ActionController::UrlFor
    include ActionController::Redirecting
    include ActionController::Rendering
    include ActionController::Renderers::All
```

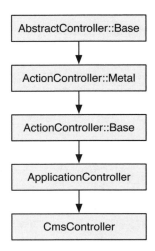

Figure 3.4: CmsController ancestors chain

```
        include ActionController::ConditionalGet
        include ActionController::RackDelegation

        # Legacy modules
        include ActionController::SessionManagement
        include ActionController::Caching
        include ActionController::MimeResponds

        # Rails 2.x compatibility
        include ActionController::Compatibility
        include ActionController::ImplicitRender

        include ActionController::Cookies
        include ActionController::Flash
        include ActionController::Verification
        include ActionController::RequestForgeryProtection
        include ActionController::Streaming
        include ActionController::RecordIdentifier
        include ActionController::HttpAuthentication::Basic::ControllerMethods
        include ActionController::HttpAuthentication::Digest::ControllerMethods

        include ActionController::Instrumentation
        include AbstractController::Callbacks
        include ActionController::Rescue
    end
end
```

How many of the previous modules do we need in our CmsController? Just a few. And this is what we are going to change. Let's reimplement CmsController, but this time inheriting from ActionController::Metal and including only the modules we need, which reduces the overhead in a request:

`templater/4_final/app/controllers/cms_controller.rb`

```
class CmsController < ActionController::Metal
  include ActionController::Rendering
  include AbstractController::Helpers

  append_view_path ::SqlTemplate::Resolver.instance
  helper CmsHelper

  def respond
    render :template => params[:page]
  end
end
```

`templater/4_final/app/helpers/cms_helper.rb`

```
module CmsHelper
end
```

After these changes, our tests should still be green, showing that our new controller implementation using ActionController::Metal works as expected.

If we need more functionality, we just need to add the required modules. For instance, if we want to add layouts, we include the AbstractController::Layouts module, create a layout in the database with the path layouts/cms, and specify layout "cms" in our controller. Try it!

3.4 Wrapping Up

We learned a lot in this chapter. We analyzed Action View's rendering stack, developed a resolver that reads templates from a database, and added caching to it. Then we created a controller to dynamically access the pages in the resolver and optimized it by making it an Action-Controller::Metal object. If you are eager to see more examples about resolvers, you can check the Rails source code and discover how it implements the filesystem resolver, which retrieves templates from the filesystem.

On the other hand, if you are already familiar with Rails' internals (such as resolvers and metal) and are still looking for a challenge, you can learn more about Ruby hashes by checking the Rubinius source code.

Rubinius implements most of the Ruby language in Ruby itself, including the Hash class, so you can learn a lot by looking through its source.

Finally, for those NoSQL lovers out there, you could also try rewriting our SqlTemplate::Resolver using another data store, such as MongoDB or CouchDB!

In the next chapter, let's discuss template handlers, such as ERb, Builder, and HAML. We will create our own handler using Markdown and ERb, and we'll hook it up into Rails' generators.

In this chapter, we'll see

- Rails template handler API
- Multipart templates with Action Mailer
- Rails generators and railties

Chapter 4

Sending Multipart Emails Using Template Handlers

To finish our tour of the Rails rendering stack, let's look at how templates are compiled and rendered by Rails. So far, we learned that a controller's responsibility is to normalize the rendering options and send them to the view context. Based on these options, the view context asks the view paths to find a template in the many resolvers it contains.

As we saw in Section 3.1, *Writing the Code*, on page 45, the resolver returns instances of ActionView::Template, and at the moment those templates are initialized, we need to pass along an object called handler as an argument. Each extension, such as .erb or .haml, has its own template handler.

The responsibility of the template handler in the rendering stack is to compile a template to Ruby source code. And to understand how this happens, let's develop a few template handlers on our own.

Our template handler aims to solve a particular issue. Even though the foundation for today's emails was created in 1970 and version 4 of the HTML specification dates from 1997, we still cannot rely on sending HTML emails to everyone since many email clients cannot render these properly.

This means that whenever we configure an application to send an HTML email, we should also send a TEXT version of the same, creating the so-called multipart email. If the email's recipient uses a client that cannot read HTML, it will fall back to the TEXT part.

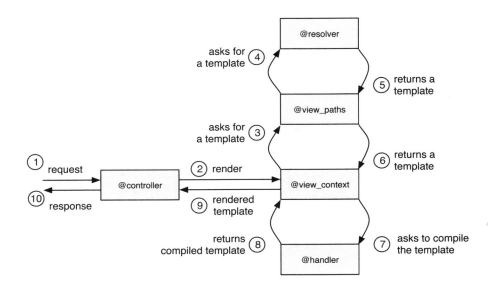

Figure 4.1: OBJECTS INVOLVED IN THE RENDERING STACK

While Action Mailer and the Mail gem make creating multipart emails a breeze, the only issue with this approach is that we have to maintain two versions of the same email message. Wouldn't it be nice if we actually have one template that could be rendered both as TEXT and as HTML?

Here's where Markdown comes in. Markdown[1] is a lightweight markup language, created by John Gruber and Aaron Swartz, that is intended to be as easy to read and easy to write as possible. Markdown's syntax consists entirely of punctuation characters and allows you to embed custom HTML whenever required. Here's an example of Markdown text:

```
Welcome
=======

Hi, José Valim!

Thanks for choosing our product. Before you use it, you just need
to confirm your account by accessing the following link:

http://example.com/confirmation?token=ASDFGHJK
```

---

1. http://daringfireball.net/projects/markdown

Welcome

Hi, José Valim!

Thanks for choosing our product. Before you use it, you just need to confirm your account by accessing the following link:

http://example.com/confirmation?token=ASDFGHJK

Remember, you have *7 days* to confirm it. For more information, you can visit our FAQ or our Customer Support page.

Regards,

The Team.

Figure 4.2: HTML GENERATED FROM A MARKDOWN TEMPLATE

```
Remember, you have *7 days* to confirm it. For more information,
you can visit our [FAQ][1] or our [Customer Support page][2].

Regards,

The Team.

[1]: http://example.com/faq
[2]: http://example.com/customer
```

Indeed, it's quite readable! The best part is that it can be transformed into HTML, which is rendered as shown in Figure 4.2.

Our template handler is going to use the features of Markdown to generate both TEXT and HTML views using just one template. The only issue with Markdown is that it does not interpret Ruby code. To circumvent this, let's first compile our templates with ERb and then convert them using the Markdown compiler.

Finally, let's also hook into the Rails 3 generators and configure the mailer generator to use our new template handler instead of ERb.

4.1 Playing with the Template Handler API

To have an object compliant with the handler API, it just needs to respond to the call method. This method receives as an argument an instance of ActionView::Template, which we already discussed in Section 3.1, *Writing the Code*, on page 45, and should return a string containing valid Ruby code. The Ruby code returned by the handler is then compiled into a method, so rendering a template is as simple as invoking this compiled method.

Before diving into our Markdown + ERb handler, let's create a few template handlers to get acquainted with the API.

Ruby Template Handler

Our first template handler simply allows arbitrary Ruby code as a template. This means the following template is valid:

```
body = ""
body << "This is my first "
body << content_tag(:b, "template handler")
body << "!"
body
```

To implement this, let's craft a new gem called handlers using enginex:

```
enginex handlers
```

Next, let's write a simple integration test for our template handler:

```
handlers/1_handlers/test/integration/navigation_test.rb
```
```ruby
require 'test_helper'

class NavigationTest < ActiveSupport::IntegrationCase
  test '.rb template handler' do
    visit '/handlers/index'
    expected = 'This is my first <b>template handler</b>!'
    assert_match expected, page.body
  end
end
```

The test makes a request to the /handlers/index path; let's define it in our router:

```
handlers/1_handlers/test/dummy/config/routes.rb
```
```ruby
Dummy::Application.routes.draw do
  get "/handlers/:action", :to => "handlers"
end
```

Since our new route points to HandlersController, let's implement it as well:

```
handlers/1_handlers/test/dummy/app/controllers/handlers_controller.rb
```
```ruby
class HandlersController < ApplicationController
end
```

And create our Ruby template at test/dummy/app/views/handlers/ index.html.rb:

`handlers/1_handlers/test/dummy/app/views/handlers/index.html.rb`

```
body = ""
body << "This is my first "
body << content_tag(:b, "template handler")
body << "!"
body
```

When we run the test suite, it fails because Rails still does not recognize the .rb extension in templates. To register a new template handler, we invoke ActionView::Template.register_template_handler with two arguments: the template extension and the handler object. Because the handler object is anything that responds to call and returns a String, we can implement our handler simply using Ruby's **lambda**. Ruby's **lambda** accepts a block and returns a Proc object that executes the given block once we invoke call and is a perfect fit because our template handler implementation is very short:

`handlers/1_handlers/lib/handlers.rb`

```
require "action_view/template"

ActionView::Template.register_template_handler :rb,
  lambda { |template| template.source }

module Handlers
end
```

Run the test suite, and the test we just wrote now passes. Our lambda receives as an argument an ActionView::Template instance. Since our template handler needs to return a String with Ruby code and our template in the filesystem is written in Ruby, we just need to return the template.source.

Because, since Ruby 1.8.7, symbols implement a to_proc method and :source.to_proc is exactly the same as lambda { |arg| arg.source }, we can make our template handler even shorter:

`handlers/1_handlers/lib/handlers.rb`

```
ActionView::Template.register_template_handler :rb, :source.to_proc
```

String Template Handler

Our .rb template handler is quite simple but has limited usage. Rails views are constituted mainly of static contents, and handling big chunks of strings in the Ruby code would quickly become messy. That said, let's implement another template handler that is more suitable to handle static content but that still allows us to embed Ruby code. Since strings in Ruby support interpolation, our next template handler will be based on strings and allow the following syntax:

handlers/2_more_handlers/test/dummy/app/views/handlers/show.html.string

```
Congratulations! You just created another #{@what}!
```

Our new template uses string interpolation, and the interpolated Ruby code references an instance variable named @what. This variable is defined in controllers and given by the view_assigns method to the view, as we discussed in Section 1.3, *Understanding Rails Rendering Stack*, on page 11. So, let's define a new action with this instance variable in our HandlersController to be used as a fixture by our tests:

handlers/2_more_handlers/test/dummy/app/controllers/handlers_controller.rb

```
class HandlersController < ApplicationController
  def show
    @what = "template handler"
  end
end
```

And write a small test for it in our integration suite:

handlers/2_more_handlers/test/integration/navigation_test.rb

```
test '.string template handler' do
  visit '/handlers/show'
  expected = 'Congratulations! You just created another template handler!'
  assert_match expected, page.body
end
```

To make our new test pass, let's implement this new template handler, once again in lib/handlers.rb, as follows:

handlers/2_more_handlers/lib/handlers.rb

```
ActionView::Template.register_template_handler :string,
  lambda { |template| "%Q{#{template.source}}" }
```

Run the test suite, and our new test passes. Our template handler returns a string created with the Ruby shortcut %Q{}, which is then compiled to a method by Rails. When this method is invoked, the Ruby interpreter evaluates the string and returns the interpolated result.

This template handler works fine for simple cases but has two major flaws: adding the } character to the template causes syntax errors unless the character is escaped, and the block support is limited, because it needs to be wrapped in the whole interpolation syntax. In other words, both of the following examples are invalid:

```
This } causes a syntax error

#{2.times do}
  This does not work as in ERb and is invalid
#{end}
```

So, let's look at more robust template handlers next.

4.2 Building a Template Handler with Markdown + ERb

Several gems can compile Markdown syntax to HTML. For our template handler, let's use RDiscount,[2] which is a Ruby wrapper to the fast Markdown compiler library called Discount, written in C.

Markdown Template Handler

Creating a template handler that can compile Markdown code is quite straightforward. Let's add another test to our suite:

`handlers/2_more_handlers/test/integration/navigation_test.rb`

```ruby
test '.md template handler' do
  visit '/handlers/rdiscount'
  expected = '<p>RDiscount is <em>cool</em> and <strong>fast</strong>!</p>'
  assert_match expected, page.body
end
```

And then let's write our template in the filesystem:

`handlers/2_more_handlers/test/dummy/app/views/handlers/rdiscount.html.md`

```
RDiscount is *cool* and **fast**!
```

Note that our template uses .md as the extension for Markdown. Let's register it in Rails:

`handlers/2_more_handlers/lib/handlers.rb`

```ruby
require "rdiscount"
ActionView::Template.register_template_handler :md,
  lambda { |template| "RDiscount.new(#{template.source.inspect}).to_html" }
```

Since our template handler relies on RDiscount, let's add it to the Gemfile and run bundle install just after:

`handlers/2_more_handlers/Gemfile`

```ruby
gem "rdiscount", "1.6.5"
```

When we run the test suite, our new test passes. While our Markdown template handler works like a charm, it does not allow us to embed

---

2. https://github.com/rtomayko/rdiscount

Ruby code, so its usage becomes quite limited. To circumvent this limitation, we could use the same technique we used in our .string template handler, but it also has its limitations when using Ruby blocks. Therefore, we are going to use ERb to embed Ruby code in our Markdown template and create a new template handler named .merb.

Markdown + ERb Template Handler

First, let's add an example of our new template handler to the filesystem. This example should be inside our dummy app and will be used in our tests:

`handlers/2_more_handlers/test/dummy/app/views/handlers/merb.html.merb`

```
MERB template handler is **<%= %w(cool fast).to_sentence %>**!
```

And then let's write a test that renders this template and check the desired output:

`handlers/2_more_handlers/test/integration/navigation_test.rb`

```ruby
test '.merb template handler' do
  visit '/handlers/merb'
  expected = '<p>MERB template handler is <strong>cool and fast</strong>!</p>'
  assert_match expected, page.body.strip
end
```

This time, to implement our template handler, we are not going to use a **lambda**. Instead, let's create a module that responds to call, so, as our implementation grows, we will be able to split and refactor it in several methods, something that would not be possible if we used a **lambda**. Also, let's use the ActionView::Template.registered_template_handler method to retrieve the ERb handler, as we did in Section 3.1, *Writing the Code*, on page 45. The code is shown here and should be added to our lib/handlers.rb file:

`handlers/2_more_handlers/lib/handlers.rb`

```ruby
module Handlers
  module MERB
    def self.erb_handler
      @@erb_handler ||= ActionView::Template.registered_template_handler(:erb)
    end

    def self.call(template)
      compiled_source = erb_handler.call(template)
      "RDiscount.new(begin;#{compiled_source};end).to_html"
    end
  end
end

ActionView::Template.register_template_handler :merb, Handlers::MERB
```

The ERb handler compiles the template, and like any other template handler, it returns a string with valid Ruby code. The result returned by this Ruby code is a String containing Markdown syntax that is then converted to HTML using RDiscount.

Finally, look how we wrapped the code returned by ERb in an inline **begin/end** clause. This must be done inline, or it will mess up backtrace lines. For instance, imagine the following template:

```
<% nil.this_method_does_not_exist! %>
```

This template obviously raises an error when rendered. However, consider those two ways to compile the template:

```
RDiscount.new(begin
  nil.this_method_does_not_exist!
end).to_html
```

```
RDiscount.new(begin;nil.this_method_does_not_exist!;end).to_html
```

In the first case, it says the error was raised in the second line, while in the latter, it correctly accuses the first line. And we need to use begin/end to wrap the code; otherwise, it's not valid Ruby code. Let's verify this by trying the following code in irb:

```
puts(a=1;b=a+1)            # => raises syntax error
puts(begin;a=1;b=a+1;end) # => prints 2 properly
```

The last line in our implementation registers our new handler, allowing all tests to pass. Our .merb template handler is already implemented, but it still does not render both TEXT and HTML templates as described at the beginning of this chapter, only the latter. So, let's change our template handler to output different results depending on the template format.

Multipart Emails

The best way to showcase the behavior we want to add to our template handler is using multipart emails in Action Mailer. So, let's create a mailer inside our dummy application to be used by our tests:

```
handlers/3_final/test/dummy/app/mailers/notifier.rb
class Notifier < ActionMailer::Base
  def contact(recipient)
    @recipient = recipient
    mail(:to => @recipient, :from => "john.doe@example.com") do |format|
      format.text
      format.html
    end
  end
end
```

The previous code should look familiar: just like respond_to in your controllers, you can give a block to mail to specify which templates to render. However in controllers, Rails chooses only one template to render, while in mailers, the block specifies several templates that are used to create a single multipart email.

Our email shown previously will have two parts, one in TEXT and another in HTML. Since both parts will use the same template, let's create a template inside our dummy app but without adding a format to its filename:

`handlers/3_final/test/dummy/app/views/notifier/contact.merb`

```
Dual templates **rocks**!
```

And let's write a test for that using this mailer and view:

`handlers/3_final/test/integration/navigation_test.rb`

```
test 'dual template with .merb' do
  email = Notifier.contact("you@example.com")
  assert_equal 2, email.parts.size
  assert_equal "multipart/alternative", email.mime_type
  assert_equal "text/plain", email.parts[0].mime_type
  assert_equal "Dual templates **rocks**!",
    email.parts[0].body.encoded.strip
  assert_equal "text/html", email.parts[1].mime_type
  assert_equal "<p>Dual templates <strong>rocks</strong>!</p>",
    email.parts[1].body.encoded.strip
end
```

The test asserts that our email has two parts. Since the TEXT part is an alternative representation of the HTML part, the email should have a MIME type equal to multipart/alternative, which is automatically set by Action Mailer. The test then proceeds by checking the MIME type and body of each part. The order of the parts is also important; if the parts were inverted, most clients would simply ignore the HTML part, showing only TEXT.

When we run this test, it fails because our text/plain part contains HTML code and not only TEXT. This is expected, since our template handler always returns HTML code. To make it pass, we will need to slightly change the implementation of Handlers::Merb.call to consider the template.formats:

`handlers/3_final/lib/handlers.rb`

```
def self.call(template)
  compiled_source = erb_handler.call(template)
  if template.formats.include?(:html)
    "RDiscount.new(begin;#{compiled_source};end).to_html"
```

```
  else
    compiled_source
  end
end
```

We inspect template.formats and check whether it includes the :html format. If so, we render the template as HTML; otherwise, we just return the code compiled by ERb, resulting in a TEXT template written in Markdown syntax. This allows us to send an email with both TEXT and HTML parts but using just one template!

With this last change, our template handler does exactly what we planned at the beginning of this chapter. Before we create generators to our new template handler, let's briefly discuss how template.formats is set.

Formats Lookup

In Section 3.1, *Writing the Code*, on page 45, you learned that the resolver is responsible for giving the :format option to templates. The resolver looks at three places to decide which format to use:

- If the template found has a valid format, it's used. In templates placed in the filesystem, the format is specified in the template filename, as in index.html.erb.

- However, if the template found does not specify a format, the resolver asks the template handler whether it has a default format.

- Finally, if the template handler has no preferred format, the resolver should return the same formats used in the lookup.

Because our contact.merb template does not specify a format, the resolver tries to retrieve the default format from our Handlers::MERB template handler. This default format is retrieved through Handlers::MERB. default_format, but since our template handler does not respond to default_format, the second step is also skipped. So, the last option to the resolver is to return the format used in the lookup. And since we are using format.text and format.html methods, they automatically set the formats in the lookup to, respectively, TEXT and HTML.

For instance, if we defined Handlers::MERB.default_format in our implementation to return :text or :html, our last test would fail, since our resolver would never reach the third step and would always return a TEXT format in the second step.

4.3 Customizing Rails Generators

With our template handler in hand and rendering multipart emails, the final step is to create a generator for our gem. Our generator will hook into Rails' mailer generator and configure it to create .merb templates instead .erb.

In versions prior to Rails 3, there was no way to partially customize a generator. If you wanted to change the templates created by the mailer generator, you had to create a whole new generator on your own, which, besides copying those new templates, should also create the mailer instance and copy test files.

So, in Rails 2.3, if both Haml and Rspec provided scaffold generators in their own gems, they couldn't work togther. If you wanted a scaffold that used both Haml and Rspec, a third generator needed to be created.

Rails 3 generators have a single responsibility and provide hooks so other generators can do the remaining work. A quick look at the mailer generator in the Rails source code reveals the hooks it provides:

rails/railties/lib/rails/generators/rails/mailer/mailer_generator.rb

```
module Rails
  module Generators
    class MailerGenerator < NamedBase
      argument :actions, :type => :array,
        :default => [], :banner => "method method"
      check_class_collision

      def create_mailer_file
        template "mailer.rb",
          File.join('app/mailers', class_path, "#{file_name}.rb")
      end

      hook_for :template_engine, :test_framework
    end
  end
end
```

Although we are not familiar with the whole Generators API yet, we can see that its main behavior is to copy a mailer template to app/mailers, which is implemented in the create_mailer_file method. Notice the mailer generator does not say anything about the template engine or the test framework; it provides only hooks. This allows Haml and Rspec developers to change Rails generators without worrying about affecting each other.

The Active Model API and the decoupling in Rails 3 generators are the major keys to agnosticism in Rails 3. We have already discussed the former in Chapter 2, *Building Models with Active Model*, on page 19, and now we are going to play with the latter.

The Structure of a Generator

To briefly describe how a generator works, let's take a deeper look at the Rails::Generators::MailerGenerator shown in the code on the facing page. The mailer generator inherits from Rails::Generators::NamedBase. All generators that inherit from it expect an argument called NAME to be given when the generator is invoked from the command line. Let's verify it by executing the following command inside a Rails application:

```
$ bundle exec rails g mailer --help
Usage:
  rails generate mailer NAME [method method] [options]

Options:
  -e, [--template-engine=NAME]  # Template engine to be invoked
                                # Default: erb
  -t, [--test-framework=NAME]   # Test framework to be invoked
                                # Default: test_unit
```

Back to our generator code. Rails::Generators::MailerGenerator, starting on line 4, defines :actions as an argument. Since a default value was provided (an empty array), these actions are optional and appear between brackets in the previous help message.

Next, the class_collisions_check method verifies that the NAME given to the generator is not already defined in our application. This is useful since it raises an error if we try to define a mailer named, for instance, Object.

On the next lines, we define the create_mailer_file method, reproduced here for convenience:

```
def create_mailer_file
  template "mailer.rb",
    File.join('app/mailers', class_path, "#{file_name}.rb")
end
```

Rails 3 generators work by invoking all public methods in the sequence they are defined. This construction is interesting because it plays well with inheritance: if you have to extend the mailer generator to do some extra tasks, you just need to inherit from it and define more public methods. Whenever your new generator is invoked, it will first execute the inherited methods and then the new public methods you defined.

As with Rails controllers, you can expose or run actions by accident by leaving a method declared as public.

The create_mailer_file method invokes three methods: template, class_path, and file_name. The first one is a helper defined in Thor,[3] which is the basis for Rails 3 generators, while the others are defined by Rails::Generators::NamedBase.

Thor has a module called Thor::Actions, which contains several methods to assist in generating tasks. One of them is the previous template method, which accepts two arguments: a source file and a destination. The template method reads the source file in the filesystem, executes the embedded Ruby code in it using ERb, and then copies the result to the given destination. All ERb templates in Thor are evaluated in the generator context, which means that instance variables defined in your generator are also available in your templates.

The values returned by the two other methods, class_path and file_name, are inflected from the NAME given as an argument. To see all the defined methods and what they return, let's sneak a peek at the named_base_test.rb file in Rails' source code:

`rails/railties/test/generators/named_base_test.rb`

```ruby
def test_named_generator_attributes
  g = generator ['admin/foo']
  assert_name g, 'admin/foo',   :name
  assert_name g, %w(admin),     :class_path
  assert_name g, 'Admin::Foo',  :class_name
  assert_name g, 'admin/foo',   :file_path
  assert_name g, 'foo',         :file_name
  assert_name g, 'Foo',         :human_name
  assert_name g, 'foo',         :singular_name
  assert_name g, 'foos',        :plural_name
  assert_name g, 'admin.foo',   :i18n_scope
  assert_name g, 'admin_foos',  :table_name
end
```

This test asserts that when admin/foo is given as NAME, as in rails g mailer admin/foo, we can access all those methods, and each of them will return the respective value given in the assertion.

Finally, the mailer generator provides two hooks: one for the template engine and another for the test framework. Those hooks become options that can be given through the command line as well. Summing it all up,

---

3. https://github.com/wycats/thor

the previous generator accepts a range of arguments and options and could be invoked as follows:

```
rails g mailer Notifier welcome contact --test-framework=rspec
```

Generators' Hooks

We already know Rails generators provides hooks. However, when we ask to use ERb as the template engine, how does the mailer generator know how to find and use it?

Generators' hooks work because of a set of conventions. When you pick a template engine named :erb, the Rails::Generators::MailerGenerator will try to load one of the following three generators:

- Rails::Generators::ErbGenerator
- Erb::Generators::MailerGenerator
- ErbGenerator

And since all generators should be in the $LOAD_PATH, under the rails/generators or the generators folder, finding these generators is as simple as trying to require the following files:

- (rails/)generators/rails/erb/erb_generator
- (rails/)generators/rails/erb_generator
- (rails/)generators/erb/mailer/mailer_generator
- (rails/)generators/erb/mailer_generator
- (rails/)generators/erb/erb_generator
- (rails/)generators/erb_generator

If one of those generators is found, it is invoked with the same command-line arguments given to the mailer generator. In this case, it defines an Erb::Generators::MailerGenerator, which we are going to discuss next.

Template Engine Hooks

Rails 3 exposes three hooks for template engines: one for the controller, one for the mailer, and one for the scaffold generators. The first two generate files only if some actions are supplied on the command line, such as in rails g mailer Notifier welcome contact or rails g controller Info about contact. For each action given, the template engine should create a template for it.

On the other hand, the scaffold hook creates all views used in the scaffold: index, edit, show, new, the _form partial, and the layout.

The implementation of Erb::Generators::ControllerGenerator in Rails is:

rails/railties/lib/rails/generators/erb/controller/controller_generator.rb

```ruby
module Erb
  module Generators
    class ControllerGenerator < Base
      argument :actions, :type => :array,
        :default => [], :banner => "action action"

      def copy_view_files
        base_path = File.join("app/views", file_path)
        empty_directory base_path

        actions.each do |action|
          @action = action
          @path    = File.join(base_path, filename_with_extensions(action))
          template filename_with_extensions(:view), @path
        end
      end
    end
  end
end
```

The only method we haven't discussed yet is filename_with_extensions, defined in Erb::Generators::Base:

rails/railties/lib/rails/generators/erb.rb

```ruby
module Erb
  module Generators
    class Base < Rails::Generators::NamedBase #:nodoc:
      protected

      def format
        :html
      end

      def handler
        :erb
      end

      def filename_with_extensions(name)
        [name, format, handler].compact.join(".")
      end
    end
  end
end
```

The Erb::Generators::ControllerGenerator creates a view file in app/views using the configured format and handler for each action given. The template used to create such views in the Rails source code looks like this:

`rails/railties/lib/rails/generators/erb/controller/templates/view.html.erb`

```
<h1><%= class_name %>#<%= @action %></h1>
<p>Find me in <%= @path %></p>
```

This, for `rails g controller admin/foo bar`, outputs the following in the file app/views/admin/foo/bar.html.erb:

```
<h1>Admin::Foo#bar</h1>
<p>Find me in app/views/admin/foo/bar</p>
```

The Erb::Generators::MailerGenerator class simply inherits from the previous controller generator and changes the default format to be :text, reusing the same logic:

`rails/railties/lib/rails/generators/erb/mailer/mailer_generator.rb`

```
module Erb
  module Generators
    class MailerGenerator < ControllerGenerator
      protected

      def format
        :text
      end
    end
  end
end
```

And the template created for mailers looks like this:

`rails/railties/lib/rails/generators/erb/mailer/templates/view.text.erb`

```
<%= class_name %>#<%= @action %>

<%%= @greeting %>, find me in app/views/<%= @path %>
```

Now let's take a glance at the ERb generator's directory structure in the Rails source code at the railties/lib directory; we can easily see which templates are available, as in Figure 4.3, on the next page.

Therefore, if we want to completely replace ERb generators, we just need to create those generators and templates. And since Rails 3 generators play well with inheritance, we can do that by inheriting from the respective ERb generator and overwriting a few configuration methods.

Creating Our First Generator

All we need to do to implement our .merb generator for the mailer is inherit from Erb::Generators::MailerGenerator and overwrite both format and handler methods defined Erb::Generators::Base. Our generator implementation looks like this:

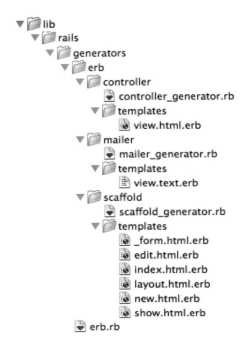

Figure 4.3: Structure for ERb generators

handlers/3_final/lib/generators/merb/mailer/mailer_generator.rb

```ruby
require "rails/generators/erb/mailer/mailer_generator"

module Merb
  module Generators
    class MailerGenerator < Erb::Generators::MailerGenerator
      source_root File.expand_path("../templates", __FILE__)

      protected
      def format
        nil # Our templates have no format
      end

      def handler
        :merb
      end
    end
  end
end
```

Note that we need to invoke a method called source_root at the class level to tell Rails where to find the template used by our generator at lib/generators/merb/mailer/templates.

Since we chose **nil** as the format and :merb as the handler, let's name our template view.merb and have the following content:

handlers/3_final/lib/generators/merb/mailer/templates/view.merb

```
<%= class_name %>#<%= @action %>

<%%= @greeting %>, find me in app/views/<%= @path %>
```

And that's it. Our template has the same contents as in the ERb generator, but you could modify it to include some Markdown by default. To try the generator, let's move to the dummy application inside our gem at test/dummy and invoke the following command:

```
bundle exec rails g mailer Mailer contact welcome --template-engine=merb
```

The previous command creates a mailer named Mailer with two templates named contact.merb and welcome.merb. The generator runs, showing us the following output:

```
create  app/mailers/mailer.rb
invoke  merb
create    app/views/mailer
create    app/views/mailer/contact.merb
create    app/views/mailer/welcome.merb
```

You can also configure your application at test/dummy/config/application.rb to use the merb generator by default, by adding the following line:

```
config.generators.mailer :template_engine => :merb
```

However, you may not want to add this line to each new application you start. It would be nice if we could set this value as the default inside our gem and not always in the application. Rails 3 allows us to do it with a Rails::Railtie. This will be our last topic before we finish this chapter.

4.4 Extending Rails with Railties

A Rails::Railtie (pronounced "Rails Rail-tie") allows you to hook into Rails' initialization and configure some defaults. In Rails 2.3, all the steps that required us to configure and initialize an application were in only one file. The lack of hooks in previous versions made it hard for other frameworks to replace Active Record, Test::Unit, and so on.

In Rails 3, the initialization process was broken apart, and several hooks were created. In this new architecture, Rails is not responsible for setting up Active Record; instead, Active Record should tell Rails how it's initialized and configured by providing its own railtie.

You should include a railtie in your gem only if at least one of the following is true:

- Your gem needs to perform a given task while or after the Rails application is initialized.

- Your gem needs to change a configuration value, such as setting a generator.

- Your gem must provide Rake tasks and generators in nondefault locations (the default location for the former is lib/tasks and lib/generators or lib/rails/generators for the latter).

- You want your gem to provide configuration options to the application, such as config.my_gem.key = :value.

Let's take a look at an excerpt of ActiveRecord::Railtie in the Rails source code that contains a few examples of these scenarios:

`rails/activerecord/lib/active_record/railtie.rb`

```ruby
module ActiveRecord
  class Railtie < Rails::Railtie
    config.active_record = ActiveSupport::OrderedOptions.new

    config.app_generators.orm :active_record, :migration => true,
                                               :timestamps => true

    config.app_middleware.insert_after "::ActionDispatch::Callbacks",
      "ActiveRecord::QueryCache"

    rake_tasks do
      load "active_record/railties/databases.rake"
    end

    initializer "active_record.initialize_timezone" do
      ActiveRecord.time_zone_aware_attributes = true
      ActiveRecord.default_timezone = :utc
    end

    initializer "active_record.set_configs" do |app|
      app.config.active_record.each do |k,v|
        ActiveRecord::Base.send("#{k}=", v)
      end
    end
  end
end
```

After such examples, we are ready to create our first railtie to configure the mailer generator to use our new template handler by default:

`handlers/3_final/lib/handlers/railtie.rb`

```ruby
module Handlers
  class Railtie < Rails::Railtie
    config.app_generators.mailer :template_engine => :merb
  end
end
```

Since our railtie must be loaded when our gem is loaded, we need to add a require in lib/handlers.rb:

`handlers/3_final/lib/handlers.rb`

```ruby
require "handlers/railtie"
```

And that's all! Let's go to the dummy application at test/dummy and invoke the generator helper once again with bundle exec rails g mailer -- help. Notice the default template engine has changed to *merb*. Therefore, we don't need to pass it as an option when invoking it!

All major Rails generators, such as model, controller, and scaffold, rely on hooks. As we've just seen, this allows us to adapt them to our workflow and preferred tools.

In Section 1.1, *Booting the Dummy Application*, on page 4, we discussed Rails' initialization process and the responsibilities of config/boot.rb and config/application.rb. Although the former is responsible for setting up the application's load path, the latter should require Rails frameworks (such as Active Record and Action Pack), load gems and extensions, and finally define and configure the application object.

The fact that gems and extensions are now loaded before the application is defined is extremely important since it allows gems to configure Rails defaults, but the application has the final word about it. For instance, we changed Rails to use our :merb template engine in the mailer generator by default. However, if developers want to set this value back to :erb, they can simply do it inside the application definition at config/application.rb.

4.5 Wrapping Up

In this chapter, we finished our discussion about Rails' rendering stack by building a couple template handlers. Our main template handler with the .merb extension mixes Markdown with ERb, allowing it to render both HTML and TEXT parts in an email by using just one template.

This functionality just works if we do not add a format to our template filename. However, if you recall the SqlTemplate::Resolver we developed in Section 3.1, *Writing the Code*, on page 45, we validate the presence of format, not allowing it to be nil. Therefore, the unique behavior of our template handler, which is rendering different results depending on the format, won't work with SqlTemplate::Resolver. Thankfully, to fix this issue, we just need to accept a format to be **nil** in the SqlTemplate class and implement inside SqlTemplate::Resolver the formats lookup described in Section 4.2, *Formats Lookup*, on page 73 so it always returns the formats used in the lookup. It's up to you to take this challenge, write some tests, and make it work![4]

Another challenge is to implement hooks for both controller and scaffold generators for our new template handler, in addition to the existing mailer generator hook. These new hooks could also be set as the default inside the Rails::Railtie, customizing them in the same way we configured the mailer to use our generator and create .merb views by default.

Finally, there is much more to discover in the Generators API. Besides the methods seen in this chapter, Thor::Actions defines copy_file, inject_into_file, empty_directory, create_file, run, and a few more. In addition, Rails has a module called Rails::Generators::Actions that provides methods specific to Rails, such as gem, environment, route, and many others. Rails also provides a testing facility to generators called Rails::Generators::TestCase, which can be handy if you need to implement generators containing some logic. You can look at Rails' test suite for some tests for the mailer generator:

`rails/railties/test/generators/mailer_generator_test.rb`

```
require 'generators/generators_test_helper'
require 'rails/generators/mailer/mailer_generator'

class MailerGeneratorTest < Rails::Generators::TestCase
  arguments %w(notifier foo bar)

  def test_mailer_skeleton_is_created
```

---

4. This new lookup should search for templates in the database with the format given on the conditions hash or where the stored format is nil. If the record has no format, Sql-Template::Resolver#initialize_template should use the default_format specified by the template handler (if the handler responds to default_format) or fall back to the format given in conditions. You can find a solution in the code folder at code/handlers/3_final/doc/sql_template.rb.

```ruby
    run_generator
    assert_file "app/mailers/notifier.rb" do |mailer|
      assert_match /class Notifier < ActionMailer::Base/, mailer
      assert_match /default :from => "from@example.com"/, mailer
    end
  end

  def test_invokes_default_test_framework
    run_generator
    assert_file "test/functional/notifier_test.rb" do |test|
      assert_match /class NotifierTest < ActionMailer::TestCase/, test
      assert_match /test "foo"/, test
      assert_match /test "bar"/, test
    end
  end

  def test_invokes_default_template_engine
    run_generator
    assert_file "app/views/notifier/foo.text.erb" do |view|
      assert_match %r(app/views/notifier/foo\.text\.erb), view
      assert_match /<%= @greeting %>/, view
    end

    assert_file "app/views/notifier/bar.text.erb" do |view|
      assert_match %r(app/views/notifier/bar\.text\.erb), view
      assert_match /<%= @greeting %>/, view
    end
  end
end
```

Be sure to explore all these tools available to you! Next, let's hook into
Rails' Notifications API to store all queries done in the database and use
a Rails engine to expose them through a web interface!

In this chapter, we'll see

- ActiveSupport::Notifications API
- Rails engines
- Rack, Rails middleware stacks, and custom middlewares
- Ruby threads and queues

Chapter 5

Managing Application Events with Rails Engines

Since Ruby on Rails' early days, people have wondered what happens inside of their applications. How many queries were performed in this request? How long did this request take?

To address this common concern, a few open source projects (such as RailsFootnotes[1] and Rack::Bug[2]) and services (such as NewRelic's RPM[3] and Scout[4]) were built. Each of them provides different features and implementations; however, they all have one thing in common: they monkey-patch Rails.

Since Rails does not provide any hooks for its internal methods, these projects and services often use alias_method_chain to instrument and collect the necessary information. An example is the following code, extracted from Rack::Bug:

```
ActiveRecord::ConnectionAdapters::AbstractAdapter.class_eval do
  def log_with_rack_bug(sql, name, &block)
    Rack::Bug::SQLPanel.record(sql, Kernel.caller) do
      log_without_rack_bug(sql, name, &block)
    end
  end

  alias_method_chain :log, :rack_bug
end
```

1. https://github.com/josevalim/rails-footnotes
2. https://github.com/brynary/rack-bug
3. http://www.newrelic.com/features.html
4. http://scoutapp.com/

The problem with this approach is that if Rails renames these methods or changes the number of arguments they receive, the tools stop working. To address this issue, Rails 3 provides a way to publish and subscribe to events happening inside your application through the Active-Support::Notifications API.

In this chapter, let's use this API to subscribe to all queries done in our application and store them in a MongoDB database. Later let's create a Rails::Engine to visualize those queries, including their duration.

5.1 Storing Notifications in the Database

Before we implement the logic to store notifications in the database, let's take a look at the Notifications API.

The Notifications API

The Notifications API is quite simple since it consists of just two methods: instrument and subscribe. The former is called when we want to instrument and publish an event, and for Active Record queries, it looks like this:

```
ActiveSupport::Notifications.instrument("sql.active_record",
  :sql => sql, :name => name, :connection_id => self.object_id) do
  connection.select_all(sql)
end
```

The first argument is the name of the event published, which in this case is sql.active_record, and the second is a hash with extra information about the event, called payload. To subscribe to those notifications, all we have to do write something like this:

```
ActiveSupport::Notifications.subscribe "sql.active_record" do |*args|
  # do something
end
```

where args is an array with five items:

- name: A String with the name of the event
- started_at: A Time object representing when the event started
- ended_at: A Time object representing when the event ended
- instrumenter_id: A String containing the unique ID of the object instrumenting the event
- payload: A Hash with the information given as payload to instrument

And that's all we need to know. Next let's take a look at the database where we are going to store the notifications.

Using MongoDB

MongoDB is a fast and document-oriented database perfectly suited to storing notifications since it's high-volume, low-value data. You can read more about MongoDB at its website,[5] which also includes installation instructions for different operating systems.

Currently, there are several ORMs to interact with MongoDB, but we are going to use MongoMapper[6] for this project. We won't cover installation instructions, so if you don't have MongoDB installed, please do it now![7] After MongoDB is installed and running, let's create a new project using enginex, called sql_metrics:

```
enginex sql_metrics
```

After Enginex creates our bare gem with a dummy application, let's add a MongoMapper model called SqlMetrics::Metric at lib/sql_metrics/metric.rb:

sql_metrics/1_setup/lib/sql_metrics/metric.rb

```
module SqlMetrics
  class Metric
    include MongoMapper::Document
  end
end
```

Next let's load the MongoMapper gem by adding it to our gem's Gemfile:

sql_metrics/1_setup/Gemfile

```
gem 'mongo_mapper', '0.8.6'
gem 'mongo', '1.1.5'
gem 'bson_ext', '1.1.5'
```

Then run bundle install. Next, let's require and set up all of our dependencies in lib/sql_metrics.rb:

sql_metrics/1_setup/lib/sql_metrics.rb

```
require "mongo_mapper"
require "sql_metrics/metric"

# We are required to choose a database name
MongoMapper.database = "sql_metrics-#{Rails.env}"
```

---

5. http://www.mongodb.org/
6. https://github.com/jnunemaker/mongomapper
7. http://www.mongodb.org/display/DOCS/Quickstart

And now our gem is MongoMapper ready! Before writing any logic that actually stores documents in the MongoDB, let's write a test at test/sql_metrics_test.rb first. The test instruments an event with the name sql and asserts a metric that was stored in MongoDB as follows:

sql_metrics/1_setup/test/sql_metrics_test.rb

```ruby
require 'test_helper'

class SqlMetricsTest < ActiveSupport::TestCase
  test "any sql. notification is saved in the mongo database" do
    payload = { "sql" => "SELECT * FROM foo" }

    ActiveSupport::Notifications.instrument "sql.any_orm", payload do
      sleep(0.001) # sleep for 1000 microseconds
    end

    metric = SqlMetrics::Metric.first
    assert_equal 1, SqlMetrics::Metric.count
    assert_equal "sql.any_orm", metric.name
    assert_equal payload, metric.payload

    assert metric.duration
    assert metric.instrumenter_id
    assert metric.started_at
    assert metric.created_at
  end
end
```

When we run the test, it fails since we are not storing anything yet:

```
1) Failure:
test_any_sql._notification_is_saved_in_the_mongo_database(SqlMetricsTest)
  <1> expected but was
<0>.
```

To make the test pass, let's first subscribe to ActiveSupport::Notifications at the end of lib/sql_metrics.rb:

sql_metrics/2_metrics/lib/sql_metrics.rb

```ruby
require "active_support/notifications"

ActiveSupport::Notifications.subscribe /^sql\./ do |*args|
  SqlMetrics::Metric.store!(args)
end
```

Our notification hook is simply calling the store! method in our SqlMetrics::Metric, which will be responsible for parsing the arguments and creating a record in the database as follows:

sql_metrics/2_metrics/lib/sql_metrics/metric.rb

```ruby
module SqlMetrics
  class Metric
    include MongoMapper::Document

    key :name, String
    key :duration, Integer
    key :instrumenter_id, String
    key :payload, Hash
    key :started_at, DateTime
    key :created_at, DateTime

    def self.store!(args)
      metric = new
      metric.parse(args)
      metric.save!
    end

    def parse(args)
      self.name            = args[0]
      self.started_at      = args[1]
      self.duration        = (args[2] - args[1]) * 1000000
      self.instrumenter_id = args[3]
      self.payload         = args[4]
      self.created_at      = Time.now.utc
    end
  end
end
```

Let's run the whole test suite once again and...see our test fail again, this time telling us that we have more than one item stored in our MongoDB database! If we debug and inspect what was stored in the database, we will see a few setup queries. This happens because Active Record does a few queries whenever we start a Rails application, and these queries are being stored by our gem. Since MongoMapper does not clean the database before tests, as Active Record does, our test is failing. To fix this, let's add a setup block that is executed before each test at the end of our test/test_helper.rb:

sql_metrics/2_metrics/test/test_helper.rb

```ruby
class ActiveSupport::TestCase
  setup { SqlMetrics::Metric.delete_all }
end
```

After this change, our test suite is green! To take a look at how our gem works outside the test environment, let's boot the application inside test/dummy and make a few SQL queries. For this, let's create a resource named User:

```
bundle exec rails generate scaffold User name:string age:integer
```

Now run the migrations, start the server, and access /users to create and edit some users. After a few requests, you can start a new console session with bundle exec rails console and see all SQL notifications created in these requests by typing SqlMetrics::Metric.all in the command line!

Although our subscriber works as expected, wouldn't it be nice if we had a page where we could see these notifications instead of using the Rails console? This page should be included in our gem, allowing everyone to visualize all SQL notifications through a nice web interface.

Let's use Rails engines to make this work!

5.2 Extending Rails with Engines

Rails engines allow our gem to have controllers, models, helpers, views, and routes, and consequently they are an excellent tool to build the notifications page. Although engines are not new in Rails 3, they had major improvements compared to previous versions.

In Rails 2.3, if you had a gem with an app folder at the gem root, all controllers, models, and views inside it were automatically pulled in, and your gem worked as an engine without any extra configuration. However, in order to make it work, Rails had to hook into Rubygems and check each gem that was loaded.

For Rails 3, we needed an explicit way to create engines, allowing it to work in any scenario, not only with Rubygems. With that in mind, Rails now ships with a new class called Rails::Engine.

To showcase how engines work, let's move the SqlMetrics::Metric model at lib/sql_metrics/metric.rb to app/models/sql_metrics/metric.rb. When you run the tests after this change, our project won't even boot, since we are requiring sql_metrics/metric, but there is no such file in the load path.

Let's fix it in two simple steps. First, let's add a Rails::Engine to our gem:

`sql_metrics/3_engine/lib/sql_metrics/engine.rb`
```
module SqlMetrics
  class Engine < Rails::Engine
  end
end
```

And second, let's require the engine at sql_metrics/engine instead of sql_metrics/metric:

```
sql_metrics/3_engine/lib/sql_metrics.rb
```
require *"sql_metrics/engine"*

Now our tests are able to run again. By defining a Rails::Engine, Rails automatically autoloads everything under the app folder inside our gem.

Creating a Rails::Engine is quite similar to creating a Rails::Railtie. This is because a Rails::Engine is nothing more than a Rails::Railtie with some default initializers and a couple more configuration options, like the Paths API.

Paths

In Rails 3, a Rails::Engine does not have hard-coded paths. This means we are not required to place our models or controllers in app/; we can put them anywhere we choose. For instance, if we want to put our controllers in lib/controllers instead of app/controllers, we need to specify it like this:

```
module SqlMetrics
  class Engine < Rails::Engine
    paths.app.controllers = "lib/controllers"
  end
end
```

We can also have Rails load our controllers from both app/controllers and lib/controllers:

```
module SqlMetrics
  class Engine < Rails::Engine
    paths.app.controllers << "lib/controllers"
  end
end
```

We are going to follow the conventional path and stick our controllers at app/controllers, so don't apply the previous changes yet. We can check all customizable paths for an engine by inspecting the Rails source code:

```
rails/railties/lib/rails/engine/configuration.rb
```
```
def paths
  @paths ||= begin
    paths = Rails::Paths::Root.new(@root)
    paths.app                  "app",     :glob => "*", :eager_load => true
    paths.app.controllers      "app/controllers",        :eager_load => true
    paths.app.helpers          "app/helpers",            :eager_load => true
    paths.app.models           "app/models",             :eager_load => true
    paths.app.mailers          "app/mailers",            :eager_load => true
```

```
    paths.app.views           "app/views"
    paths.lib                 "lib",                     :load_path => true
    paths.lib.tasks           "lib/tasks",               :glob => "**/*.rake"
    paths.config              "config"
    paths.config.initializers "config/initializers", :glob => "**/*.rb"
    paths.config.locales      "config/locales",          :glob => "*.{rb,yml}"
    paths.config.routes       "config/routes.rb"
    paths.public              "public"
    paths.public.javascripts  "public/javascripts"
    paths.public.stylesheets  "public/stylesheets"
    paths
  end
end
```

Initializers

An engine has several initializers that are responsible for making the engine work. Here is one of them:

`rails/railties/lib/rails/engine.rb`

```
initializer :add_routing_paths do |app|
  paths.config.routes.to_a.each do |route|
    app.routes_reloader.paths.unshift(route) if File.exists?(route)
  end
end
```

This initializer receives a Rails::Application object, like the one defined in every Rails application at config/application.rb, and adds the engine routes, at config/routes.rb, to the routes reloader. To see all initializers defined in a Rails::Engine, we can start a new Rails console under test/dummy with bundle exec rails console and type the following:

```
Rails::Engine.initializers.map(&:name) # => [
  :set_load_path, :set_autoload_paths, :add_routing_paths,
  :add_routing_namespaces, :add_locales, :add_view_paths, :add_metals,
  :load_config_initializers, :load_app_classes
]
```

These initializers are responsible for running through the defined paths and adding locales files to I18n, appending view paths to Action Controller and Action Mailer, loading metals, and so forth.

Working with an engine is pretty much the same as working with a Rails application. Since we know how to build applications, building the notifications page should be straightforward.

The Notifications Page

Before we implement the notifications page, let's write an integration test at test/integration/navigation_test.rb that creates a user executing a few queries in the database and asserts that /sql_metrics exhibits these queries:

sql_metrics/3_engine/test/integration/navigation_test.rb

```ruby
require 'test_helper'

class NavigationTest < ActiveSupport::IntegrationCase
  test 'can visualize and destroy notifications created in a request' do
    visit new_user_path
    fill_in "Name", :with => "John Doe"
    fill_in "Age", :with => "23"
    click_button "Create User"

    # Check for the metric data on the page
    visit sql_metrics_path
    assert_match "User Load", page.body
    assert_match "INSERT INTO", page.body
    assert_match "John Doe", page.body
    assert_match "sql.active_record", page.body

    # Assert the number of rows change when an item is destroyed
    assert_difference "all('table tr').count", -1 do
      click_link "Destroy"
    end
  end
end
```

To create our notifications page, let's create a controller, a view, and routes inside our gem. Let's start with the controller:

sql_metrics/3_engine/app/controllers/sql_metrics_controller.rb

```ruby
class SqlMetricsController < ApplicationController
  def index
    @metrics = SqlMetrics::Metric.all
  end

  def destroy
    @metric = SqlMetrics::Metric.find(params[:id])
    @metric.destroy
    redirect_to sql_metrics_url
  end
end
```

Our controller has two actions: index and destroy. For the first one, we need to create a view:

sql_metrics/3_engine/app/views/sql_metrics/index.html.erb

```erb
<h1>Listing SQL Metrics</h1>

<table cellspacing="10">
  <tr>
    <th>Name</th>
    <th>Duration</th>
```

```erb
      <th>Started at</th>
      <th>Payload</th>
      <th></th>
    </tr>

<% @metrics.each do |metric| %>
  <tr>
    <td><%= metric.name %></td>
    <td><%= metric.duration %>us</td>
    <td><%= time_ago_in_words metric.started_at %> ago</td>
    <td>
      <% metric.payload.each do |k, v| %>
        <p><b><%= k.humanize %></b><br /> <%= v %></p>
      <% end %>
    </td>
    <td><%= link_to 'Destroy', sql_metric_path(metric),
        :confirm => 'Are you sure?', :method => :delete %></td>
  </tr>
<% end %>
</table>
```

Then, let's add some routes at config/routes.rb:

`sql_metrics/3_engine/config/routes.rb`

```ruby
Rails.application.routes.draw do
  resources :sql_metrics, :only => [:index, :destroy]
end
```

Run the test and watch it pass! Notice it automatically runs all migra-tions before executing the test suite, since it is configured to do so inside test/test_helper.rb:

```ruby
ActiveRecord::Migrator.migrate(
  File.expand_path("../dummy/db/migrate/", __FILE__)
)
```

To see everything working, let's move to the application in test/dummy, start the server, access /sql_metrics, and see all the notifications that we saw in the Rails console earlier.

With these changes, our gem now provides a model, a controller, a view, and routes, all handled by Rails!

5.3   Rails and Rack

We are able to store SQL notifications in the database, but it may be useful to not store notifications for certain requests. For instance, if we have an admin panel, it may be unnecessary to store notifications happening inside the admin section.

To achieve this, let's develop middleware that sets a flag in SqlMetrics, turning it off for a specific request. But before we dive into the code, let's first take a look at how deeply Rails 3 integrates Rack.

What Is Rack?

> Rack provides a minimal, modular, and adaptable interface for developing web applications in Ruby. By wrapping HTTP requests and responses in the simplest way possible, it unifies and distills the API for web servers, web frameworks, and software in between (the so-called middleware) into a single method call.
>
> —Rack documentation[8]

Rails applications need a web server in order to interact through the HTTP protocol. And since the early days, the Rails community saw a huge range of web servers available to deploy their applications.

Before Rack, Rails was responsible for providing an adapter to each different web server it supported: one for Mongrel, another for WEBrick, another for Thin, and so on. Similarly, the MERB team, since they had a different API than Rails, had to provide different adapters for the same web servers.

This quickly proved to be a duplication of efforts, and at the beginning of 2007, when the Ruby community saw the biggest range of alternative web frameworks, Rack came out proposing a unified API. By following the Rack API, a web framework could use Rack web servers adapters instead of providing its own, removing the duplication of effort existing in the Ruby community.

While Rails 2.2 already provided a simple Rack interface, Rails more closely embraced Rack and its API in version 2.3. However, the Rack revolution really happened in Rails 3, where several parts of Rails became Rack end points, and you could easily mount different Rack applications in the same process. For example, we can easily mount a Sinatra application inside the Rails router, as we will see in the following chapters.

---

8. http://rack.rubyforge.org/doc/

Hello, Rack!

The Rack specification clearly outlines the API used by Rack applications to communicate with a web server and between themselves:

> A Rack application is a Ruby object (not necessarily a class) that responds to call. It takes exactly one argument, the environment, and returns an array of exactly three values: the status, the headers, and the body.
>
> —Rack specification[9]

Rack's minimal API allows us to write a simple web application in just a few lines of code:

```ruby
require 'rubygems'
require 'rack'

class HelloRack
  def call(env)
    [200, { 'Content-Type' => 'text/html' }, 'Hello Rack!']
  end
end

run HelloRack.new
```

By creating the previous config.ru file in a directory and invoking the rackup command inside this same directory, Rack starts a web server and invokes our HelloRack application in each request. When you fire up a browser and hit http://localhost:9292/, you can see "Hello Rack!" returned as the response body.

All Rails 3 applications ship with a config.ru file, as we can see in the dummy application inside test/dummy with the following contents:

```ruby
# This file is used by Rack-based servers to start the application.

require ::File.expand_path('../config/environment',  __FILE__)
run Dummy::Application
```

In other words, the Dummy::Application defined inside test/dummy/config/application.rb is a Rack application and can be initialized on its own.

Middleware Stacks

Although web server adapters and the Rack application API revolutionized the way that Ruby web frameworks are developed, you are probably more familiar with another term related to Rack: *middleware*.

---

9. http://rack.rubyforge.org/doc/files/SPEC.html

Middleware sits between the web server and the Rack application. It lets us manipulate both the request sent down to the application and the response returned by the application. However, if a Rack application contains another Rack application, you may also use middleware to modify the request-response life cycle internally. By piling up middleware, we create a so-called *middleware stack*. Any request to an action in a Rails 3 controller passes at least through three middleware stacks.

The first of these three middleware stacks is hidden by Rails. It sits between the web server and the Rails::Application object and contains only two middleware components:

- Rails::Rack::LogTailer: It parses the log file and prints it on console.

- Rails::Rack::Debugger: It requires and enables ruby-debug.

After passing through this middleware stack, the request hits a Rails:: Application (for example our Dummy::Application inside test/dummy), which is nothing more than another middleware stack with the router sitting at the end.

The stack contained by the Rails::Application is the most known middleware stack in Rails and has been available since version 2.3. You can add or remove middleware from this stack through config.middlewares available inside config/application.rb. To see all available middleware in the stack, we need to invoke rake middleware from the command line at the application root.

For our dummy application inside test/dummy, this command returns exactly the following:

```
use ActionDispatch::Static
use Rack::Lock
use ActiveSupport::Cache::Strategy::LocalCache
use Rack::Runtime
use Rails::Rack::Logger
use ActionDispatch::ShowExceptions
use ActionDispatch::RemoteIp
use Rack::Sendfile
use ActionDispatch::Callbacks
use ActiveRecord::ConnectionAdapters::ConnectionManagement
use ActiveRecord::QueryCache
use ActionDispatch::Cookies
use ActionDispatch::Session::CookieStore
use ActionDispatch::Flash
use ActionDispatch::ParamsParser
use Rack::MethodOverride
use ActionDispatch::Head
run Dummy::Application.routes
```

Part of the Rails 3 refactoring involved moving some responsibilities (including cookies, sessions, and flash middleware) from the controller to the middleware stack. Besides these three, Rails provides other middleware that can be used stand-alone in any Rack application:

- ActiveSupport::Cache::Strategy::LocalCache: Uses an in-memory cache store to provide a local cache during requests
- ActionDispatch::ShowExceptions: Is responsible for showing helpful error pages in development and rendering status pages in production from the public directory
- ActionDispatch::RemoteIp: Handles IP spoof checking
- ActionDispatch::Callbacks: Runs the so-called to_prepare callbacks, which happens once on application boot in production and before each request in development (such as I18n reloading and observers loading)
- ActionDispatch::ParamsParser: Parses the parameters given in the request, both from query string or in the POST body
- ActionDispatch::Head: Converts HEAD requests to GET requests

Your ORM of choice will likely add a few middleware to the stack as well. In our case, we can see both ConnectionManagement and QueryCache from Active Record. If you were using DataMapper, you would see a middleware related to IdentityMap.

The last group of middleware comes from Rack itself and is shared between frameworks:

- Rack::Lock: Synchronizes non-thread-safe requests
- Rack::Runtime: Measures the request time and returns it as an X-Runtime header
- Rack::Sendfile: Implements X-Sendfile header for different web servers
- Rack::MethodOverride: Checks POST requests and converts them to PUT or DELETE if _method is present in parameters

The last stop in the stack is the application router, which is yet another Rack application. If the router dispatches the request to a specific action in a controller, it will also pass through another middleware stack. Since Rails 3, each controller also has its own middleware stack to which we can add a middleware with the following syntax:

```
class UsersController < ApplicationController
  use MyMiddleware
  use AnotherMiddleware
end
```

This middleware is invoked before the action is called and before any filters, so it sits quite high in the controller stack. It seems we have more than one place that we can put our middleware to turn off SqlMetrics, so let's implement it!

MuteMiddleware

Before writing our middleware, we need to ensure SqlMetrics provides an API to mute notifications for a specific block of code. A proposed API is shown in the test here:

```
sql_metrics/4_mute/test/sql_metrics_test.rb
```

```ruby
test 'can ignore notifications when specified' do
  SqlMetrics.mute! do
    assert SqlMetrics.mute?

    ActiveSupport::Notifications.instrument "sql.any_orm" do
      sleep(0.001) # sleep for 1000 microseconds
    end
  end

  assert !SqlMetrics.mute?
  assert_equal 0, SqlMetrics::Metric.count
end
```

This API relies on two methods: mute! and mute?. The former receives a block, and all notifications happening inside the block should not be stored in the database. The latter returns a boolean depending whether we are in a mute block.

To make the previous test pass, we implement these two methods, as shown here:

```
sql_metrics/4_mute/lib/sql_metrics/mute_middleware.rb
```

```ruby
module SqlMetrics
  def self.mute!
    Thread.current["sql_metrics.mute"] = true
    yield
  ensure
    Thread.current["sql_metrics.mute"] = false
  end

  def self.mute?
    Thread.current["sql_metrics.mute"] || false
  end
end
```

Notice we used thread variables to ensure that muting a request in a thread is not going to affect other threads in a threaded environment.

Also, we need to wrap the yield call in an **ensure** block, allowing the mute status to be reverted even if an exception happens while executing the block (you should write a test case for this scenario and ensure it works as expected).

After we implement mute! and mute?, we need to change lib/sql_metrics.rb to load lib/sql_metrics/mute_middleware.rb and the ActiveSupport::Notifications hook to not store notifications if mute? returns **true**. After these changes, the file should look like the following:

`sql_metrics/4_mute/lib/sql_metrics.rb`

```ruby
require "active_support/notifications"
require "mongo_mapper"
require "sql_metrics/mute_middleware"
require "sql_metrics/engine"

# We are required to choose a database name
MongoMapper.database = "sql_metrics-#{Rails.env}"

ActiveSupport::Notifications.subscribe /^sql\./ do |*args|
  SqlMetrics::Metric.store!(args) unless SqlMetrics.mute?
end
```

Run the tests again, and verify that our mute API works as expected.

Now let's write the middleware that uses it to mute a whole request, starting by the test. The test asserts two behaviors related to a new method called mute_regexp= that accepts a regexp specifying which paths should be muted. If mute_regexp is **nil**, we do not mute any request, and all metrics are stored. However, if we set mute_regexp= to %r{^/users}, all paths starting with /users won't have their notifications stored in the database. Our test goes like this:

`sql_metrics/4_mute/test/integration/navigation_test.rb`

```ruby
test 'can ignore notifications for a given path' do
  assert_difference "SqlMetrics::Metric.count" do
    visit "/users"
  end

  begin
    SqlMetrics.mute_regexp = %r{^/users}
    assert_no_difference "SqlMetrics::Metric.count" do
      visit "/users"
    end
  ensure
    SqlMetrics.mute_regexp = nil
  end
end
```

The previous test won't pass because there is no mute_regexp= method defined. The configuration method and middleware implementations are exhibited next:

`sql_metrics/4_mute/lib/sql_metrics/mute_middleware.rb`

```ruby
module SqlMetrics
  mattr_accessor :mute_regexp
  @@mute_regexp = nil

  class MuteMiddleware
    def initialize(app)
      @app = app
    end

    def call(env)
      if SqlMetrics.mute_regexp && env["PATH_INFO"] =~ SqlMetrics.mute_regexp
        SqlMetrics.mute!{ @app.call(env) }
      else
        @app.call(env)
      end
    end
  end
end
```

However, this is not enough to make our test pass since we need to register our middleware in the application middleware stack. Luckily, this is easy to achieve in both Rails::Railtie and Rails::Engine:

`sql_metrics/4_mute/lib/sql_metrics/engine.rb`

```ruby
module SqlMetrics
  class Engine < Rails::Engine
    # Insert the mute middleware high in the stack to ensure
    # no queries in the stack will escape the mute.
    config.app_middleware.insert_after "ActionDispatch::Callbacks",
      "SqlMetrics::MuteMiddleware"

    # Make configurations proxy to SqlMetrics module
    config.sql_metrics = SqlMetrics
  end
end
```

The config object exposes the application middleware stack (the one that ends up in the router) through the app_middleware method. We insert our middleware high in the stack, because we may have middleware in the stack doing SQL queries besides the application. A common example is the Sessions middleware, which may do some queries if the session store is the database.

Since our SqlMetrics module now provides a configuration option, we also set the sql_metrics option in the config object. This allows us to configure our gem from inside config/application.rb through a nice API:

```
class Application < ::Rails::Application
  config.sql_metrics.mute_regexp = %r{^/admin}
end
```

After all these changes, our test suite is green once again, showing our middleware is functional and has a nice configuration API! Way to go!

MuteMiddleware in Other Stacks

In the previous section, we added our middleware to the middleware stack that ends up in the router. But as we know, Rails 3 provides other middleware stacks, so the question is, can we use our middleware in any of them?

Rails does not expose the first middleware stack, the one between the web server and the Rails::Application object. Mainly, there isn't a need for it. And when it comes to the controller middleware stack, we could indeed include our middleware, but we need to reevaluate its implementation a bit.

Our middleware allows us to configure the path it should mute through a regular expression. However, when we are in the controller, we already passed through the router, so we don't want the middleware to consider the current path. Instead, we want to mute the whole controller, independent of the path the request was made. A more adequate implementation of a mute middleware for controllers would be as follows:

```
class MuteControllerMiddleware
  def initialize(app)
    @app = app
  end

  def call(env)
    SqlMetrics.mute!{ @app.call(env) }
  end
end
```

And then we simply declare it in our controller:

```
class AdminController < ApplicationController
  # You could also use :only and :except options.
  # use MuteControllerMiddleware, :only => :index
  use MuteControllerMiddleware
end
```

It's up to you to try it! It's important to remember, though, that this functionality could also be achieved using the prepend_around_filter method in controllers:

```ruby
class AdminController < ApplicationController
  prepend_around_filter :mute_notifications

  protected

  def mute_notifications
    SqlMetrics.mute!{ yield }
  end
end
```

Ruby and Rails provides several options to achieve the same behavior. Choose the one that suits you better!

5.4 Storing Notifications Asynchronously

At this point, we can successfully store and visualize all SQL notifications happening inside our application and mute undesired ones. However, if a request does ten SQL queries, the request has an extra overhead of ten insertions done in MongoDB. The need to move some processing to the background is very common to Rails applications, and there are several solutions.

Let's take a look at one possible solution for this common problem next.

Threads and Queues

Let's create an in-process queue that stores the arguments yielded by ActiveSupport::Notification.subscribe. This queue is consumed by a thread, which stores these notifications in MongoDB.

To implement the solution described, we'll rely solely on the Ruby Standard Library since Ruby ships with an in-process Queue implementation. A queue is first-in first-out data structure and therefore has a very simple API:

```ruby
require "thread"
q = Queue.new

t = Thread.new do
  while last = q.pop
    sleep(1) # simulate expense
    puts last
  end
end
```

```
q << :foo
sleep(1)
$stdout.flush
```

The previous code creates a new Queue and a new Thread. Inside the thread there is a loop that calls Queue#pop. If there is no item in the queue, the thread will block until an item is pushed to the queue. In the last three lines, we push a symbol to the queue, which will wake up the thread. After one second, if we flush what was pushed to $stdout, we can see "foo" printed. If we have several threads blocking on the queue, the queue manages to wake up one thread at a time to consume the queue.

This means we can change ActiveSupport::Notifications.subscribe to push all notifications to the queue, and, at startup, we will create a thread to consume this queue and save the items in the queue to MongoDB.

Async Subscriptions

To make our implementation behave asynchronously, let's rewrite the block given to ActiveSupport::Notifications.subscribe. The file at lib/sql_metrics.rb should look like this:

sql_metrics/5_final/lib/sql_metrics.rb

```
require "active_support/notifications"
require "mongo_mapper"
require "sql_metrics/mute_middleware"
require "sql_metrics/engine"
require "thread"

# We are required to choose a database name
MongoMapper.database = "sql_metrics-#{Rails.env}"

module SqlMetrics
  def self.queue
    @queue ||= Queue.new
  end

  def self.thread
    @thread ||= Thread.new do
      while args = queue.pop
        SqlMetrics::Metric.store!(args)
      end
    end
  end
end
```

```
# Start the Queue and Thread
SqlMetrics.queue
SqlMetrics.thread

ActiveSupport::Notifications.subscribe /^sql\./ do |*args|
  SqlMetrics.queue << args unless SqlMetrics.mute?
end
```

Now run the tests with our new implementation, and they may pass...or not! Depending on your machine, the tests may always pass or always fail or alternate between failing and passing. This happens because saving documents to the MongoDB happens asynchronously, so sometimes the test assertions may happen before the documents are saved to the database and will consequently fail.

To work around this situation, we need a way to ensure the thread finished storing items in MongoDB. We could do this by calling SqlMetrics.thread.join, but this won't work in our case because our thread never finishes; it always blocks in the queue, and calling SqlMetrics.thread.join would lead to a deadlock, which is a situation where two threads are waiting each other to finish, but none of them will.

In other words, we need a way to tell our thread to finish by finishing the while loop. And if we pay attention closely, there is already a way. If we push **nil** to the queue, the while args = queue.pop expression will evaluate to false, and the loop will be aborted. That said, let's implement a finish! method inside SqlMetrics with the following:

sql_metrics/5_final/lib/sql_metrics.rb

```
def self.finish!
  queue << nil
  thread.join
  @thread = nil
  thread
end
```

The method pushes a **nil** object to the queue. Then we call thread.join, which will consume all items in the queue and finish the thread once the nil object is consumed. However, after the thread is finished, we need to create a new one, so the following notifications are still consumed. To do so, we set the @thread instance variable to **nil** and call the thread method once again, creating another consumer thread.

Now, to ensure our tests will always pass, let's invoke SqlMetrics.finish! after each ActiveSupport::Notifications.instrument call in our unit test. Here is one example:

sql_metrics/5_final/test/sql_metrics_test.rb

```
ActiveSupport::Notifications.instrument "sql.any_orm" do
  sleep(0.001) # sleep for 1000 microseconds
end

SqlMetrics.finish!
```

The integration tests should call finish! just after the form is submitted:

sql_metrics/5_final/test/integration/navigation_test.rb

```
click_button "Create User"
SqlMetrics.finish!
```

and each time after the /users path is requested:

sql_metrics/5_final/test/integration/navigation_test.rb

```
visit "/users"
SqlMetrics.finish!
```

Now our tests always pass, and our implementation does not block the request when storing notifications in MongoDB!

5.5 Wrapping Up

In this chapter, we developed a Rails engine that listens to all SQL events published in an application and stores them in MongoDB. These notifications can be seen by accessing /sql_metrics in the browser.

Our implementation uses an in-process queue, allowing these notifications to be stored asynchronously. Although the implementation is quite straightforward, the queue provides no persistence; thus, if the process dies, all items in the queue that were not yet consumed are going to be lost. In our case, losing a few instrumentation events does not represent an issue.

Finally, there is still a lot to be done in our gem when it comes to the visualization part. We could, for instance, allow the developer to sort these metrics by duration and provide charts. And since we have all queries stored, it would be nice if we could run EXPLAIN in some queries to identify why they are not performing well.

Engine Yard provides a tool called RailsMetrics,[10] which is similar to the one we developed, but it stores all notifications that happen inside your application, not just SQL ones. It provides charts per request and other tools, which you may be interested in checking out and helping improve!

Next, let's learn how to encapsulate our controllers' behavior in an object called ActionController::Responder and customize it to suit our needs! Then we'll discuss Rails generators and learn other ways to customize Rails 3 generators.

---

10. https://github.com/engineyard/rails_metrics

- Rails responders and the respond_with method
- Rails generators' templates customization

Chapter 6

Writing DRY Controllers
with Responders

Rails' scaffold generator is a great tool to help us prototype a new application, and it became even more flexible in Rails 3. The only problem with scaffolding is that the generated controllers are still a little bit verbose, and we end up with a lot of behavior duplicated across different controllers. For example, here are the index, show, and create actions for the UsersController generated in scaffold:

```ruby
class UsersController < ApplicationController
  def index
    @users = User.all

    respond_to do |format|
      format.html # index.html.erb
      format.xml  { render :xml => @users }
    end
  end

  def show
    @user = User.find(params[:id])

    respond_to do |format|
      format.html # show.html.erb
      format.xml  { render :xml => @user }
    end
  end

  def create
    @user = User.new(params[:user])

    respond_to do |format|
```

```ruby
      if @user.save
        format.html {
          redirect_to(@user, :notice => 'User was successfully created.')
        }
        format.xml {
          render :xml => @user, :status => :created, :location => @user
        }
      else
        format.html { render :action => "new" }
        format.xml {
          render :xml => @user.errors, :status => :unprocessable_entity
        }
      end
    end
  end
end
```

All of these respond_to blocks are very similar from one controller to another. To solve this issue, Rails 3 introduced a new method called respond_with, which uses an ActionController::Responder to abstract how our controllers respond. That said, using this new syntax, these actions are reduced to the following:

```ruby
class UsersController < ApplicationController
  respond_to :html, :xml

  def index
    @users = User.all
    respond_with(@users)
  end

  def show
    @user = User.find(params[:id])
    respond_with(@user)
  end

  def create
    @user = User.new(params[:user])
    flash[:notice] = 'User was successfully created.' if @user.save
    respond_with(@user)
  end
end
```

We declare at the top which formats our controller responds to and delegate all the hard work to respond_with. We could rewrite all of our actions using this cleaner syntax.

In this chapter, we'll learn how responders work, customize them to handle HTTP caching and flash messages automatically, and finally customize the scaffold generator to use respond_with by default.

6.1 Understanding Responders

To understand the concepts behind responders, we must understand the three variables that affect how controllers respond: request type, HTTP verb, and resource status.

Navigational and API Requests

A controller generated by the scaffold generator responds to two formats by default: HTML and XML. The reason why scaffold uses these two formats is because they represent two types of requests: navigational and API requests. The former is the one handled by a browser and holds formats like HTML and IPHONE, while the latter is used by machines and represents formats like XML and JSON.

```
def index
  @users = User.all

  respond_to do |format|
    format.html # index.html.erb
    format.xml  { render :xml => @users }
  end
end
```

Let's analyze the index action the scaffold generator created for us. The HTML format receives no block, so it renders a template, while the XML format renders the XML representation of the resource with render :xml => @users.

This means that, depending on the request type, controllers behave in one way or another. Consequently, in order to abstract how controllers work, responders should take the request type into account.

HTTP Verb

As we continue analyzing the actions in the scaffolded controller, we see that the next two actions, show and new, behave exactly the same as the index action for the same request types. For navigational requests, like HTML, they render a template, and for API requests, like XML, they render the resource.

```
def show
  @user = User.find(params[:id])

  respond_to do |format|
    format.html # show.html.erb
    format.xml  { render :xml => @user }
  end
end
```

```
def new
  @user = User.new

  respond_to do |format|
    format.html # new.html.erb
    format.xml  { render :xml => @user }
  end
end
```

This behavior only changes in the create action. So, what do the index, show, and new actions have in common that the create action does not? The HTTP verb.

If the HTTP verb is GET, our controller responds in one way. If it's POST, PUT, or DELETE, it behaves in a completely different fashion. In other words, the HTTP verb is another variable that affects how the scaffolded controller responds.

At this point, it is also important to note the edit action does not respond to XML formats. This is because the edit page is used only by navigational requests and consequently does not use respond_with as well.

Finally, to better summarize the scaffolded controller behavior, we are going to create a table representing how it responds depending on the request type and HTTP verb:

	Navigational	API
GET	render template	render resource.to_format
POST	—	—
PUT	—	—
DELETE	—	—

So far, we know how it responds for GET in both request types. Now let's run through these other HTTP verbs and fill this whole table.

Resource Status

If we analyze the create action, which represents a POST request, we realize that it has two branches: one if the resource is saved with success and the other if not. Each of these branches responds in a different way:

```
def create
  @user = User.new(params[:user])

  respond_to do |format|
    if @user.save
```

```
      format.html {
        redirect_to(@user, :notice => 'User was successfully created.')
      }
      format.xml {
        render :xml => @user, :status => :created, :location => @user
      }
    else
      format.html { render :action => "new" }
      format.xml {
        render :xml => @user.errors, :status => :unprocessable_entity
      }
    end
  end
end
```

The status of the resource determines how the scaffolded controller responds. In this case, we redirect if the resource saves but render a page with errors if saving fails. We can also see this pattern in the update action, which is invoked by PUT requests.

Although the destroy action generated by the scaffolding does not seem to depend on the resource status, we may eventually need to change the destroy action to handle cases where resource.destroy returns false. For example, imagine a setup where a group has several managers. Because a group needs to have at least one manager, we implement a before_destroy callback that checks for this condition every time we try to remove a manager. If the condition isn't met, both the callback and the destroy method return false. This new scenario needs to be handled in the controller, usually by changing the destroy action to show a flash message and redirect to the group page. In other words, even though the destroy action generated by the scaffold does not depend on the resource status, DELETE requests may depend on it.

That said, the controller needs to know the resource status in order to respond to POST, PUT, and DELETE requests. Our table is modified to represent this new scenario. And with all three variables that affect our controller behavior specified, we can now fill in the table, as shown in Figure 6.1, on the next page. This table represents exactly how our controller behaves depending on the request type, HTTP verb, and resource status. All respond_with does is call ActionController::Responder, which is nothing more than this whole table written in Ruby code.

Next, let's explore how ActionController::Responder is implemented and how we can modify it to behave in a custom way.

		Navigational	API
GET		render template	render resource.to_format
POST	Success	redirect_to resource	render resource.to_format, :status => :created
POST	Failure	render :new	render resource.errors, :status => :unprocessable_ entity
PUT	Success	redirect_to resource	head :ok
PUT	Failure	render :edit	render resource.errors, :status => :unprocessable_ entity
DELETE	Success	redirect_to collection	head :ok
DELETE	Failure	redirect_to collection	render resource.errors, :status => :unprocessable_ entity

Figure 6.1: SCAFFOLD RESOURCE BEHAVIOUR

6.2   Exploring ActionController::Responder

Anything that responds to call, accepting three arguments, can be a responder. This means you can use **lambda** to create a responder. The three arguments given in the initialization are the current controller, the resource (or a nested resource or an array of resources), and a hash of options. All the options given to respond_with are forwarded to the responder as the third argument.

The ActionController::Responder implements the call method in a single line of code, as we can see in Rails source code:

rails/actionpack/lib/action_controller/metal/responder.rb

```
def self.call(*args)
  new(*args).respond
end
```

The call method just forwards these three arguments to the ActionController::Responder initialization and then calls respond:

```
rails/actionpack/lib/action_controller/metal/responder.rb
```

```ruby
# Main entry point for responder responsible to dispatch
# to the proper format.
def respond
  method = :"to_#{format}"
  respond_to?(method) ? send(method) : to_format
end

# HTML format does not render the resource, it always attempt
# to render a template.
def to_html
  default_render
rescue ActionView::MissingTemplate => e
  navigation_behavior(e)
end

# All other formats follow the procedure below. First we try to render a
# template, if the template is not available, we verify if the resource
# responds to :to_format and display it.
def to_format
  default_render
rescue ActionView::MissingTemplate => e
  api_behavior(e)
end
```

The respond method checks whether the responder responds to the current request format. If positive, it calls the specific method for this format; otherwise, it calls to_format. Since ActionController::Responder defines only to_html, only HTML requests have a custom behavior, and all others fall back to the to_format case.

By analyzing both to_html and to_format implementations, we can clearly see that the former responds with navigational_behavior and the latter with api_behavior. If we add a new navigational format to an application, like IPHONE, the responder will treat it as an API format and not navigational. Luckily, because of how responders work, we can make IPHONE use the navigational behavior by simply aliasing the :to_iphone method to :to_html in an initializer.

```ruby
ActionController::Responder.class_eval do
  alias :to_iphone :to_html
end
```

Additionally, note that a responder always invokes the default_render method before falling back to the API or navigational behavior. The default_render simply tries to render a template, and in case the template is not found, it raises an ActionView::MissingTemplate, which is properly rescued, allowing responders behavior to kick in.

The navigational_behavior and api_behavior implementation comes next:

```
rails/actionpack/lib/action_controller/metal/responder.rb
```
```ruby
ACTIONS_FOR_VERBS = {
  :post => :new,
  :put => :edit
}

# This is the common behavior for "navigation" requests, like
# :html, :iphone and so forth.
def navigation_behavior(error)
  if get?
    raise error
  elsif has_errors? && default_action
    render :action => default_action
  else
    redirect_to resource_location
  end
end

# This is the common behavior for "API" requests, like :xml and :json.
def api_behavior(error)
  raise error unless resource.respond_to?(:"to_#{format}")

  if get?
    display resource
  elsif has_errors?
    display resource.errors, :status => :unprocessable_entity
  elsif post?
    display resource, :status => :created, :location => resource_location
  else
    head :ok
  end
end

# Display is just a shortcut to render a resource with the current format.
#
#   display @user, :status => :ok
#
# For XML requests it's equivalent to:
#
#   render :xml => @user, :status => :ok
#
# Options sent by the user are also used:
#
#   respond_with(@user, :status => :created)
#   display(@user, :status => :ok)
#
```

```
# Results in:
#
#   render :xml => @user, :status => :created
#
def display(resource, given_options={})
  controller.render given_options.merge!(options).merge!(format => resource)
end

# Check whether the resource has errors.
def has_errors?
  resource.respond_to?(:errors) && !resource.errors.empty?
end

# By default, render the <code>:edit</code> action for HTML requests
# with failure, unless the verb is POST.
def default_action
  @action ||= ACTIONS_FOR_VERBS[request.request_method_symbol]
end
```

The navigational_behavior implementation is easy to read and maps straight to the table in Section 6.1, *Resource Status*, on page 114. For a GET request, it raises a missing template error, because the only option for GET requests is to render a template, which we already tried and did not succeed.

For other HTTP verbs, the navigational behavior checks whether the resource has errors. If positive and a default action is given, it renders the default action specified by the ACTIONS_FOR_VERBS hash. Finally, if the resource does not have errors, it redirects to the resource, which is what we expect in success cases.

The api_behavior implementation goes through a different path. Notice that it makes use of the display method, which merges the options given to respond_with and adds a format before calling render. In other words, when we call respond_with like this:

```
respond_with @user, :status => :created
```

on GET requests for XML format, the controller responds as follows:

```
render :xml => @user, :status => :created
```

It's important to realize Rails responders do not call @user.to_xml. They simply delegate this responsibility to the render method and consequently to the :xml renderer, as we saw in Section 1.2, *Writing the Renderer*, on page 7! This is important because people can add new renderers, and they work in responders without adding any other line of code.

Finally, the last customization available in responders can be done in our own controller. Imagine that we have a responder that works great in all cases, except for one specific action and format where we want it to behave differently. How can we change it? We can use the same syntax as in respond_to:

```
def index
  @users = User.all
  respond_with(@users) do |format|
    format.xml { render :xml => @users.to_xml(:some_specific_option => true) }
  end
end
```

And this all works because respond_with forwards the block given to format.xml to the responder when the request format is XML. This block, whenever available, is called in the default_render method shown earlier.

The great advantage in using ActionController::Responder is that it centralizes how our application should behave per format. That said, if we want to change how all controllers behave at once, we just need to create our own responder and configure Rails to use it, as shown here:

```
ApplicationController.responder = MyAppResponder
```

Furthermore, we can even set custom responders for specific controllers in our application:

```
class UsersController < ApplicationController
  self.responder = MyCustomUsersResponder
end
```

Let's create a responder with some extra behavior and ask Rails to use it.

6.3 The Flash Responder

The scaffolded controller uses flash messages in both create and update actions. These messages are quite similar across different controllers. Wouldn't it be nice then if we could set these flash messages by default inside responders but still provide a nice API to change them?

Let's implement this feature next using I18n. I18n provides a nice lookup API and also uses a YAML file, which is the perfect place for us to keep our flash messages. Let's use enginex to create a new project called responders:

```
enginex responders
```

Let's start by writing a test case that performs all CRUD actions and ensure a flash message is being exhibited to the client:

responders/1_setup/test/integration/navigation_test.rb

```ruby
require 'test_helper'

class NavigationTest < ActiveSupport::IntegrationCase
  test 'sets flash messages automatically' do
    visit "/users"

    click_link "New User"
    fill_in "Name", :with => "John Doe"
    click_button "Create User"

    assert has_content?("User was successfully created."),
      "Expected to show flash message on create"

    click_link "Edit"
    fill_in "Name", :with => "Doe, John"
    click_button "Update User"

    assert has_content?("User was successfully updated."),
      "Expected to show flash message on update"

    click_link "Back"
    click_link "Destroy"

    assert has_content?("User was successfully destroyed."),
      "Expected to show flash message on destroy"
  end
end
```

The test accesses the /users path, which can be generated by invoking the scaffold generator inside the dummy application at test/dummy.

```
bundle exec rails g scaffold User name:string
```

However, the scaffold generator does not use the responder syntax. So, let's change the generated controller to use respond_with, removing all flash messages from the controller as well, because they will be set by the responders:

responders/1_setup/test/dummy/app/controllers/users_controller.rb

```ruby
class UsersController < ApplicationController
  respond_to :html, :xml

  def index
    @users = User.all
    respond_with(@users)
  end
```

```ruby
  def show
    @user = User.find(params[:id])
    respond_with(@user)
  end

  def new
    @user = User.new
    respond_with(@user)
  end

  def edit
    @user = User.find(params[:id])
  end

  def create
    @user = User.new(params[:user])
    @user.save
    respond_with(@user)
  end

  def update
    @user = User.find(params[:id])
    @user.update_attributes(params[:user])
    respond_with(@user)
  end

  def destroy
    @user = User.find(params[:id])
    @user.destroy
    respond_with(@user)
  end
end
```

When we run the test suite, it fails with the following message:

```
1) Error:
test_sets_flash_messages_automatically(NavigationTest):
  Expected to show flash message on create.
  <false> is not true.
```

The failure is expected because our application layout does not show any flash messages and we haven't implemented our responder yet. Let's fix the former:

responders/2_responders/test/dummy/app/views/layouts/application.html.erb

```erb
<p class="notice"><%= notice %></p>
<p class="alert"><%= alert %></p>
```

Let's now create the basis for our responder and set it as the default in ActionController::Base:

`responders/1_setup/lib/responders.rb`

```ruby
module Responders
  class AppResponder < ActionController::Responder
  end
end

ActionController::Base.responder = Responders::AppResponder
```

The responder basis still does not have any logic related to flash messages. This is because we will implement it in a module called Responders::Flash that will do the lookup in the I18n framework for a message to be set in the flash hash.

Imagine a request with valid parameters at the create action in the UsersController. When respond_with is called and no flash message is set, the responder should try to find an I18n message under the controller namespace and action, which in this case is "flash.users.create.notice". If an I18n message is found, the responder should set it in flash[:notice], and it will be properly exhibited in the next request.

Alternatively, if the request at UsersController#create does not have valid parameters (that is, the created user is invalid), the responder should search for a message at "flash.users.create.alert" and set flash[:alert] instead.

With these constraints in mind, let's write our Responders::Flash module:

`responders/2_responders/lib/responders/flash.rb`

```ruby
module Responders
  module Flash
    def to_html
      set_flash_message! unless get?
      super
    end

    def set_flash_message!
      status = has_errors? ? :alert : :notice
      return if controller.flash[status].present?

      namespace = controller.controller_path.gsub("/", ".")
      action    = controller.action_name

      lookup  = [namespace, action, status].join(".").to_sym
      default = ["actions", action, status].join(".").to_sym
```

```
      i18n_options = {
        :scope => :flash,
        :default => default,
        :resource_name => resource.class.model_name.human
      }

      message = I18n.t(lookup, i18n_options)
      controller.flash[status] = message if message.present?
    end
  end
end
```

Our module overwrites the to_html behavior to set flash messages for non-GET requests and then calls **super**, allowing the responder behavior and other extensions to kick in.

Besides setting flash messages based in the controller namespace, our implementation gives an "actions" namespace as a :default option to I18n.t. This allows I18n to fall back to "flash.actions.create.notice" if a message cannot be found at "flash.users.create.notice".

This fallback mechanism allows us to provide application-wide default messages so we don't need to repeat ourselves in each controller. Let's set the default scaffold messages inside our gem by simply creating a YAML file with the following:

responders/2_responders/lib/responders/locales/en.yml

```yaml
en:
  flash:
    actions:
      create:
        notice: "%{resource_name} was successfully created."
        alert: ""
      update:
        notice: "%{resource_name} was successfully updated."
        alert: ""
      destroy:
        notice: "%{resource_name} was successfully destroyed."
        alert: "%{resource_name} could not be destroyed."
```

Now any controller will by default use the flash messages configured in this YAML file, unless a specific key for the controller is given. To achieve this, we use I18n interpolation, which allows us to use %{resource_name} in our messages, and it will be properly replaced by the resource human name given to :resource_name when I18n.t is invoked.

Before running our tests again, let's include Responders::Flash in Responder::AppResponder and configure the I18n framework to use the default messages specified in the previous YAML file:

responders/2_responders/lib/responders.rb

```
require "responders/flash"

module Responders
  class AppResponder < ActionController::Responder
    include Flash
  end
end

ActionController::Base.responder = Responders::AppResponder

require 'active_support/i18n'
I18n.load_path << File.expand_path('../responders/locales/en.yml', __FILE__)
```

Run the test suite and see that our responder is properly triggered and is using the default flash messages in the YAML file! Since our first test asserts only for "notice" messages, let's write one more test asserting that "alert" messages will be shown in case of failures.

responders/2_responders/test/integration/navigation_test.rb

```
test 'read alert messages from the controller scope' do
  begin
    I18n.backend.store_translations :en,
      :flash => { :users => { :destroy => { :alert => "Cannot destroy!" } } }

    visit "/users"

    click_link "New User"
    fill_in "Name", :with => "Undestroyable"
    click_button "Create User"

    click_link "Back"
    click_link "Destroy"

    assert has_content?("Cannot destroy!"),
      "Expected to show flash message on destroy"
  ensure
    I18n.reload!
  end
end
```

The test creates a resource and tries to destroy it but fails, showing a message that the resource cannot be destroyed. As we did in Section 2.1, *Aiming for an Active Model–Compliant API*, on page 24, we're using the I18n API to store translations on the fly for the failure scenario.

To make the test pass, we need to make @user.destroy return **false**. This is done by adding a callback that adds error messages to @user.errors and returns false if the username is "Undestroyable":

responders/2_responders/test/dummy/app/models/user.rb

```ruby
class User < ActiveRecord::Base
  before_destroy do
    if self.name == "Undestroyable"
      self.errors.add(:base, "is undestroyable")
      false
    end
  end
end
```

With this final change, our tests pass again! There are other features we could add to our flash responder, but let's move on and make our responder a better HTTP citizen.

6.4 HTTP Cache Responder

Rails 1.2 is where Rails started to embrace REST, and since then, developing APIs has become easier and easier. However, as your application grows, you may have to focus more on your API implementation and find ways to optimize the number of requests it can handle.

When you expose an API, it's common that a client requests a resource to the server several times, and the client always gets the same response back since the requested resource has not changed. In these cases, the server is wasting time rendering the same resource all over again, and the client is parsing the same response just to find out that nothing has changed.

Luckily, the HTTP 1.1 specification has a section dedicated to caching. The previous problem could be easily solved if the server appends a Last-Modified header to the response with a timestamp representing when the resource was last modified. For subsequent requests, the client should add an If-Modified-Since header with this timestamp, and if the resource has not changed, the server should return a 304 Not Modified status and does not need to render the resource again. Upon receiving a 304 status, the client knows that nothing has changed. This scenario is exhibited in Figure 6.2, on the next page.

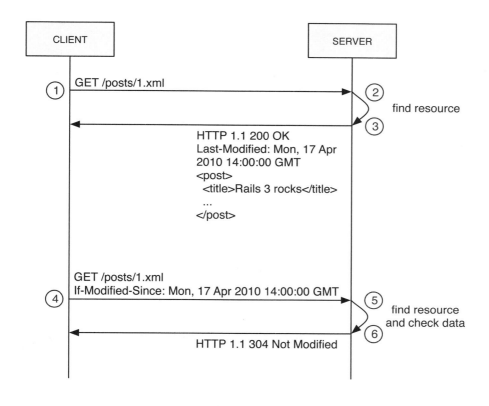

Figure 6.2: CLIENT AND SERVER INTERACTION WITH HTTP CACHE

As usual, let's start our implementation by writing tests first. There are at least three scenarios to take into account:

- When If-Modified-Since is not provided, our controller responds normally but adds a Last-Modified header.

- When If-Modified-Since is provided and fresh, our controller responds with a status of 304 and a blank body.

- When If-Modified-Since is provided and not fresh, our controller responds normally but adds a new Last-Modified header.

To write these tests, we need to modify some request headers and verify that a few response headers are being properly set. For this reason, we cannot use Capybara, since it hides the request and response objects from us (as any integration test suite should). Instead, let's use

ActionController::TestCase, the built-in structure in Rails to write functional tests.

All three scenarios are tested here using the UsersController as a fixture:

responders/3_http_cache/test/http_cache_test.rb

```ruby
require 'test_helper'

class HttpCacheResponderTest < ActionController::TestCase
  tests UsersController

  def setup
    @request.accept = "application/xml"
    ActionController::Base.perform_caching = true

    # Create two resources to be used in :index actions
    User.create(:name => "First", :updated_at => Time.utc(2009))
    User.create(:name => "Second", :updated_at => Time.utc(2008))
  end

  def test_responds_with_last_modified_using_the_latest_timestamp
    get :index
    assert_equal Time.utc(2009).httpdate, @response.headers["Last-Modified"]
    assert_match '<?xml version="1.0" encoding="UTF-8"?>', @response.body
    assert_equal 200, @response.status
  end

  def test_returns_not_modified_if_request_is_still_fresh
    @request.env["HTTP_IF_MODIFIED_SINCE"] = Time.utc(2009, 6).httpdate
    get :index
    assert_equal 304, @response.status
    assert @response.body.blank?
  end

  def test_returns_ok_with_last_modified_if_request_is_not_fresh
    @request.env["HTTP_IF_MODIFIED_SINCE"] = Time.utc(2008, 6).httpdate
    get :index
    assert_equal Time.utc(2009).httpdate, @response.headers["Last-Modified"]
    assert_match '<?xml version="1.0" encoding="UTF-8"?>', @response.body
    assert_equal 200, @response.status
  end
end
```

Rails 2.3 introduced several helpers on top of the HTTP Cache specification, and we are simply going to use them to create a new module called Responders::HttpCache that automatically adds HTTP Cache to all GET requests:

responders/3_http_cache/lib/responders/http_cache.rb

```ruby
module Responders
```

```ruby
module HttpCache
  delegate :response, :to => :controller

  def to_format
    return if do_http_cache? && do_http_cache!
    super
  end

  protected

  def do_http_cache!
    response.last_modified ||= max_timestamp if max_timestamp
    head :not_modified if fresh = request.fresh?(response)
    fresh
  end

  # Iterate through all resources and find the last updated.
  def max_timestamp
    @max_timestamp ||= resources.flatten.map do |resource|
      resource.updated_at.try(:utc) if resource.respond_to?(:updated_at)
    end.compact.max
  end

  # Just trigger the cache if it's a GET request and perform
  # caching is enabled.
  def do_http_cache?
    get? && ActionController::Base.perform_caching
  end
end
end
```

Our implementation mainly loops through all given resources and retrieves the timestamp of the last updated one. We then update the response object, and if the request is fresh (that is, if the resource was not modified), we return a 304 status to the client and do not render any resource, since to_format returns before calling **super**.

Before running our new tests, let's add Responders::HttpCache to our AppResponder, modifying the top of the lib/responders.rb file:

`responders/3_http_cache/lib/responders.rb`

```ruby
require "responders/flash"
require "responders/http_cache"

module Responders
  class AppResponder < ActionController::Responder
    include Flash
    include HttpCache
  end
end
```

And that's it! Our test suite is green again! We extracted the flash and HTTP Cache responsibility from our controllers, and now it's handled automatically by our responder. The best of all is that each feature was added in just a few lines of code!

6.5 More Ways to Customize Generators

Now that we understand how responders really work and how to adapt them to our needs, we feel confident about using them more and more in our controllers. The only issue is that the scaffold generator uses respond_to by default and not respond_with.

On the other hand, we learned in Section 4.3, *Generators' Hooks*, on page 77 how to customize generators, and there must be a hook to customize the controller generated in scaffold, right? To confirm our thoughts, we just need to take a look at the output generated by the scaffold:

```
  invoke  active_record
  create    db/migrate/20100412155054_create_posts.rb
  create    app/models/post.rb
   route  resources :posts
  invoke  scaffold_controller
  create    app/controllers/posts_controller.rb
  invoke    erb
  create      app/views/posts
  create      app/views/posts/index.html.erb
  create      app/views/posts/edit.html.erb
  create      app/views/posts/show.html.erb
  create      app/views/posts/new.html.erb
  create      app/views/posts/_form.html.erb
  invoke    helper
  create      app/helpers/posts_helper.rb
  invoke  stylesheets
identical    public/stylesheets/scaffold.css
```

Each invoke in the output is a hook that we can overwrite. This means we can indeed replace scaffold_controller generator by another one that fits our needs.

However, this is not how we will solve this problem. Instead, let's use another feature provided by Rails 3 generators that allows us to customize generator templates without a need to use generator hooks.

Generators' Source Path

Consider the following line in a Rails 3 generator:

```
copy_file "controller.rb", "app/controller/#{file_name}_controller.rb"
```

It simply copies the controller.rb file from the generators' source to the given destination, which for a UsersController would be app/controllers/users_controller.rb.

What we haven't discussed so far is that a generator does not have only one source but several. Before copying a file to a given location, the generator searches for this source file in several locations, called *source paths*. The source_root class method we specified in Section 4.3, *Creating Our First Generator*, on page 79 is actually the last place a generator searches for a template.

This behavior is actually built into Thor, but Rails 3 wraps it nicely by automatically adding the lib/templates directory inside your application to all generators' source paths. This means that the Rails::Generators::ScaffoldControllerGenerator used in scaffold will always try to find a template at lib/templates/rails/scaffold_controller before using the one provided by Rails.

When we look at Rails::Generators::ScaffoldControllerGenerator implementation in Rails source code, we can easily see the logic that copies the controller template:

rails/railties/lib/rails/generators/rail . . . troller/scaffold_controller_generator.rb

```
module Rails
  module Generators
    class ScaffoldControllerGenerator < NamedBase
      def create_controller_files
        template "controller.rb", File.join("app/controllers", class_path,
          "#{controller_file_name}_controller.rb")
      end
    end
  end
end
```

It uses a template named controller.rb, which is available at railties/lib/rails/generators/rails/scaffold_controller/templates/controller.rb. According to the source paths, if we place a file at lib/templates/rails/scaffold_controller/controller.rb inside our application, Rails will use this application file instead of the one that ships with Rails!

You can easily try this by creating a new Rails application, placing an empty file at lib/templates/rails/scaffold_controller/controller.rb inside your application, and running the scaffold command. When you check the controller created by the scaffold, it's empty as well!

Next, let's use this awesome feature to customize scaffold to use respond_with by default.

Using respond_with by Default

To use respond_with by default in the scaffold, let's place a template inside our application's lib/templates. However, to avoid doing this in each new application, we are going to create a generator that copies a file to the proper location.

Let's call this generator Responders::Generators::InstallGenerator and implement it as follows:

responders/4_final/lib/generators/responders/install/install_generator.rb

```ruby
module Responders
  module Generators
    class InstallGenerator < Rails::Generators::Base
      source_root File.expand_path("../templates", __FILE__)

      def copy_template_file
        copy_file "controller.rb",
          "lib/templates/rails/scaffold_controller/controller.rb"
      end
    end
  end
end
```

The template used by our generator is exhibited next:

responders/4_final/lib/generators/responders/install/templates/controller.rb

```ruby
class <%= controller_class_name %>Controller < ApplicationController
  respond_to :html, :xml

<% unless options[:singleton] -%>
  def index
    @<%= table_name %> = <%= orm_class.all(class_name) %>
    respond_with(@<%= table_name %>)
  end
<% end -%>

  def show
    @<%= file_name %> = <%= orm_class.find(class_name, "params[:id]") %>
    respond_with(@<%= file_name %>)
  end

  def new
    @<%= file_name %> = <%= orm_class.build(class_name) %>
```

```
    respond_with(@<%= file_name %>)
  end

  def edit
    @<%= file_name %> = <%= orm_class.find(class_name, "params[:id]") %>
  end

  def create
    @<%= file_name %> = <%=orm_class.build(class_name,"params[:#{file_name}]")%>
    @<%= orm_instance.save %>
    respond_with(@<%= file_name %>)
  end

  def update
    @<%= file_name %> = <%= orm_class.find(class_name, "params[:id]") %>
    @<%= orm_instance.update_attributes("params[:#{file_name}]") %>
    respond_with(@<%= file_name %>)
  end

  def destroy
    @<%= file_name %> = <%= orm_class.find(class_name, "params[:id]") %>
    @<%= orm_instance.destroy %>
    respond_with(@<%= file_name %>)
  end
end
```

The previous template is based on the one that ships with Rails, but it replaces all respond_to calls with respond_with. Note it also uses several methods we have already discussed, except orm_class and orm_instance, which we are going to discuss soon.

To try a new generator, you can simply move to the dummy application and invoke it:

```
bundle exec rails g responders:install
```

Now when you scaffold any new resource, it uses the new template! This means the Rails scaffold is flexible not only for Rails extensions like Haml or Rspec but also for application developers because they can customize scaffold to fit their workflow and their application structure and markup.

Generators and ORM Agnosticism

We already discussed Active Model and its role in ORM agnosticism. We also talked about generator hooks, which provide a way for other ORMs to hook into model and scaffold generators. However, there is one element we haven't discussed yet.

Rails controllers are responsible for interacting with the model and passing the desired objects to the view. In other words, controllers should interact with the current ORM and retrieve the required information from it. The controller generated by scaffolding should change depending on the ORM used.

Since previous Rails versions were not prepared to deal with ORM agnosticism, every new ORM library had to create another scaffold generator in order to hook into Rails, duplicating all the controller code. Rails 3 solves this problem by creating an object responsible to tell the scaffold generator how the interaction with the ORM happens. The basic implementation for this object is available in the Rails source code, and it looks like this:

rails/railties/lib/rails/generators/active_model.rb

```ruby
module Rails
  module Generators
    class ActiveModel
      attr_reader :name

      def initialize(name)
        @name = name
      end

      # GET index
      def self.all(klass)
        "#{klass}.all"
      end

      # GET show
      # GET edit
      # PUT update
      # DELETE destroy
      def self.find(klass, params=nil)
        "#{klass}.find(#{params})"
      end

      # GET new
      # POST create
      def self.build(klass, params=nil)
        if params
          "#{klass}.new(#{params})"
        else
          "#{klass}.new"
        end
      end

      # POST create
      def save
```

```
        "#{name}.save"
      end

      # PUT update
      def update_attributes(params=nil)
        "#{name}.update_attributes(#{params})"
      end

      # POST create
      # PUT update
      def errors
        "#{name}.errors"
      end

      # DELETE destroy
      def destroy
        "#{name}.destroy"
      end
    end
  end
end
```

The orm_class simply points to Rails::Generators::ActiveModel, and orm_instance points to an instance of this same class. So, whenever we invoke orm_class.all("User") in the template, it invokes Rails::Generators::Active-Model.all("User") and returns User.all, which is the normal Active Record behavior.

The orm_instance behaves similarly, except we don't need to pass the resource name as an argument, since we already did it in initialization. So, orm_instance.save successfully returns user.save for Active Record.

All interaction between the controller and the ORM is specified in Rails::Generators::ActiveModel. The agnosticism comes from the fact that any ORM can provide its own implementation of this class. All we need to do is to define an Active Model class inside the ORM's generator namespace.

For example, DataMapper has different syntax for finding and updating records. So, it needs to inherit from Rails::Generators::ActiveModel and implement the new API:

```
module DataMapper
  module Generators
    class ActiveModel < ::Rails::Generators::ActiveModel
      def self.find(klass, params=nil)
        "#{klass}.get(#{params})"
      end
```

```
    def update_attributes(params=nil)
      "#{name}.update(#{params})"
    end
  end
 end
end
```

This structure provided by generators plus the Active Model API is what makes agnosticism possible in Rails 3 and allows any developer to choose the ORM they find most appropriate for their work.

6.6 Wrapping Up

In this chapter, we looked into responders to understand how they work and how to customize them. As a proof of concept, we developed two extensions for responders, one to handle flash messages and another to handle HTTP caching.

There is much more we could delegate to responders. In the HTTP layer, we could use the If-Unmodified-Since request-header to provide conditional PUT requests, wherein the resource is updated only if not modified after the given date; otherwise, we return a 409 Conflict status. This scenario is exhibited in Figure 6.3, on the facing page.

We also took another look at Rails 3 generators and learned more about ORM agnosticism.

If you want to bring responders and respond_with to your workflow, you may want to try the Responders gem by Plataforma Tec,[1] which implements both extensions developed in this chapter with some extra functionalities, such as the ability to change responders to redirect to the index action instead of the show action when a user is created or updated.

Next, let's create a Rails application that allows us to translate I18n messages through a Sinatra app authenticated with Devise, a popular authentication library.

---

1. https://github.com/plataformatec/responders

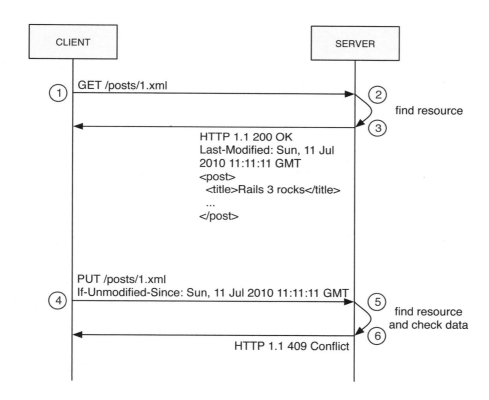

Figure 6.3: CLIENT AND SERVER INTERACTION WITH HTTP CONDITIONAL REQUESTS

In this chapter, we'll see

- The I18n framework
- The Sinatra web framework
- The Rails router
- Devise (for authentication) and Capybara (for integration testing) gems

Chapter 7

Translating Applications Using Key-Value Backends

Added in Rails 2.2, the internationalization framework (I18n) definitely played a key role in increasing Rails adoption around the world. Although we can easily make an application available in different languages, the biggest issue is to maintain this translation data. Some have a team of translators available, while others choose a collaborative approach and allow their own users to translate the web app. In both cases, asking these translators to work with the YAML files directly is not a viable solution, so it is common to develop a web interface to do these kinds of changes.

Although we could easily implement a web interface that allows users to translate our application, using YAML files to store these translations would require a mechanism to tell all servers to sync and reload these YAML files once they are updated. As you can imagine, such a solution could grow in complexity quickly.

Luckily, the I18n framework comes with different backends that allow us to store translations in other places than YAML files. For example, since version 0.3.0 of the I18n gem, we can retrieve translations from Active Record. This makes it much easier to manipulate the translations table through a web interface and update the site translations on demand. There is no need to synchronize YAML files between web servers. On the downside, retrieving translations from the database instead of an in-memory hash causes a huge impact in performance.

A solution that can comply with both these requirements (simplicity and performance) is a key-value store. In this chapter, we will store translations in a Redis store and use a Key Value backend to retrieve them. Additionally, we will build a simple Sinatra[1] application to expose a web interface to read, create, and update these translations on the fly.

Unlike previous chapters, all this functionality won't be developed as a gem but as a Rails application. After studying and analyzing railties and engines, we can now build Rails applications with a different perspective.

7.1 Revisiting Rails::Application

In Section 5.2, *Extending Rails with Engines*, on page 92, we discussed Rails::Engine and how it exhibits several behaviors similar to a Rails application. When we look at Rails source code, we find the following:

```
module Rails
  class Application < Engine
    # ...
  end
end
```

In fact, the Rails::Application class inherits from Rails::Engine! This means an application can do everything an engine does, plus some specific behavior:

- An application is responsible for all bootstrapping (for example, loading Active Support, setting up load paths, configuring the logger, and so on).

- An application has its own router and middleware stack (as we discussed in Section 5.3, *Middleware Stacks*, on page 98).

- An application should load and initialize railties, engines, and plug-ins.

- An application is responsible for reloading routes between requests if they changed.

- An application is responsible for loading tasks and generators when appropriate.

---

1. http://www.sinatrarb.com/

To take a closer look at these responsibilities, let's start developing our Translator app:

```
rails new translator
```

By opening config/environment.rb, we see that it simply loads the application definition and calls initialize! in the application object. initialize! is responsible for booting the application, including all railties, engines, and plug-ins. This method is not defined in engines, since they cannot boot on their own.

Another behavior exclusive to the Rails::Application object is in the Rakefile:

```
# Add your own tasks in files placed in lib/tasks ending in .rake,
# and they will automatically be available to Rake.

require File.expand_path('../config/application', __FILE__)
require 'rake'

Translator::Application.load_tasks
```

Although load_tasks, differently from initialize!, is defined in both Rails::Application and Rails::Engine, calling it in an engine loads only the engine Rake tasks, while calling it in an application loads all the application tasks, including the ones for engines, railties, and plug-ins.

Finally, let's look at config.ru in the root of our application. We can see that a Rails application is a valid Rack application (in other words, it defines a call method that receives a hash and returns an array with status, headers, and response body):

```
# This file is used by Rack-based servers to start the application.

require ::File.expand_path('../config/environment', __FILE__)
run Translator::Application
```

The Translator::Application#call method simply invokes the middleware stack we discussed in Section 5.3, *Middleware Stacks*, on page 98, with the router sitting at the end. Since we now understand the application responsibilities and how it is built on top of railties and engines, it is time to move back to the Translator app and create our translation back-end using the I18n API.

7.2 I18n Backends and Extensions

Whenever we invoke I18n.translate (also aliased as I18n.t) or I18n.localize (also aliased as I18n.l) in our application, it is in fact just delegating these methods to the I18n backend stored in I18n.backend. By replacing this backend, you can completely modify how the I18n library works. The I18n framework has four different backends:

- I18n::Backend::Simple: Is the default backend and keeps translations in an in-memory hash populated from YAML files

- I18n::Backend::ActiveRecord: Uses Active Record to retrieve translations from the database (moved from the I18n framework to an external gem[2] since I18n 0.5 version)

- I18n::Backend::KeyValue: Uses any key value store as backend, as long it complies with a minimum API

- I18n::Backend::Chain: Allows you to chain several backends; in other words, if a translation cannot be found in one backend, it searches for it in the next backend in the chain

In Rails 2.3, the I18n::Backend::Simple was the only functionality used by default by Rails from I18n. However, in Rails 3, a few changes were introduced. When you start a new Rails application, you can see the first one in config/environments/production.rb in the following line:

```
config.i18n.fallbacks = true
```

Whenever this configuration option is set to true, Rails configures the I18n framework to *include* the fallbacks functionality in the current backend, allowing any translation to fall back to the default locale if one cannot be found in the current locale. If you are using I18n outside of a Rails application, you can also use the fallbacks behavior with one line of code:

```
I18n.backend.class.send(:include, I18n::Backend::Fallbacks)
```

The second I18n feature used by Rails 3 is transliteration support. The transliteration that ships with Rails allows you to replace accented Latin characters with their correspondent unaccented ones, as shown here:

```
I18n.transliterate("olé") # => "ole"
```

---

2. https://github.com/svenfuchs/i18n-active_record

If you need to transliterate Hebraic, Cyrillic, Chinese characters, and so on, you can add new transliteration rules on demand. Keep in mind that fallbacks and transliterations are not a backend but one of the several extensions provided by the I18n library listed here:

- I18n::Backend::Cache: Uses a cache store in front of I18n.t to store translation results, that is, the string after lookup, interpolation, and pluralization took place
- I18n::Backend::Cascade: Cascades lookups by removing nested scopes from the lookup key; in other words, if :"foo.bar.baz" cannot be found, it automatically searches for :"foo.bar";
- I18n::Backend::Cldr: Provides support to CLDR (the common locale data repository)
- I18n::Backend::Fallbacks: Provides locale fallbacks, falling back to the default locale if a translation cannot be found in the current one
- I18n::Backend::Gettext: Provides support to gettext and .po files
- I18n::Backend::InterpolationCompiler: Compiles interpolation keys (like %{model}) into translation data to speed up performance
- I18n::Backend::Memoize: Memoizes lookup results; opposed to I18n::Backend::Cache, it uses an in-memory hash and is useful if you are using key-value or Active Record backends
- I18n::Backend::Metadata: Adds metadata (such as pluralization count and interpolation values) to translation results
- I18n::Backend::Pluralization: Adds support to pluralization rules under :"i18n.plural.rule"
- I18n::Backend::Transliterator: Adds support to transliteration rules (as discussed earlier) under :"i18n.transliterate.rule";

The I18n library provides several backends and extensions for different areas such as improving performance or adding more flexibility for languages with specific needs. In this chapter, though, we are going to use just two of them: I18n::Backend::KeyValue and I18n::Backend::Memoize.

The Key Value backend for I18n can accept any object as a store as long as it complies with the following API:

- @store[]: A method to read a value given a key
- @store[]=: A method to set a value given a key
- @store.keys: A method to retrieve all stored keys

Since providing a compliant API is trivial, almost all key-values wrappers in Ruby can be used with this backend, as Redis,[3] Riak,[4] Tokyo Cabinet,[5] and so on. In this chapter, let's use Redis because it is quite easy to install.

After Redis is installed and running, let's integrate it with our Rails application by adding the redis[6] gem, a pure-Ruby client library for Redis, to our Gemfile:

translator/1_translator/Gemfile

```
gem "redis", "2.1.1"
```

And then install it:

```
bundle install
```

Now let's fire up a Rails console with bundle exec rails console and check that Redis conforms with the API expected by I18n:

```
db = Redis.new
db["foo"] = "bar"
db["foo"] # => bar
db.keys   # => ["foo"]
```

Going back to our I18n setup, let's create a file called lib/translator.rb, which will be responsible for setting up a Redis instance pointing to the appropriate database (the database is referenced as an integer in Redis). Let's also create a customized Key Value backend that includes the I18n::Backend::Memoize module to cache lookups and uses the Redis store on initialization:

translator/1_translator/lib/translator.rb

```
module Translator
  DATABASES = {
    "development" => 0,
    "test" => 1,
    "production" => 2
  }

  def self.store
    @store ||= Redis.new(:db => DATABASES[Rails.env.to_s])
  end
```

---

3. http://code.google.com/p/redis/
4. http://riak.basho.com/
5. http://1978th.net/tokyocabinet/
6. https://github.com/ezmobius/redis-rb

```ruby
  class Backend < I18n::Backend::KeyValue
    include I18n::Backend::Memoize

    def initialize
      super(Translator.store)
    end
  end
end
```

Next, let's configure the I18n framework to use our new backend at Translator::Application:

`translator/1_translator/config/application.rb`

```ruby
module Translator
  class Application < Rails::Application
    # Set translator backend for I18n
    require "translator"
    config.i18n.backend = Translator::Backend.new
```

Opposed to the default I18n backend, both the Active Record and Key Value backends do not load translations from YAML files before each request but just on demand (since it would be slow). That said, to store all default translations in our Redis store, we just need to execute the following command in a terminal:

```
bundle exec rails runner "I18n.backend.load_translations"
```

When we start the Rails console once again, we can access all new translations stored in our Redis store:

```ruby
db = Translator.store
db.keys
db["en.errors.messages.blank"]
```

Notice that, as promised, the messages were properly stored in JSON!

7.3 Rails and Sinatra

With translations properly stored, we can now write our Translator app using Sinatra. Sinatra is a DSL for quickly creating web applications in Ruby with minimal effort. The "Hello world" is just a few lines of code:

```ruby
# myapp.rb
require 'sinatra'

get '/' do
  'Hello world!'
end
```

In our case, we won't access the Sinatra application directly, but we'll integrate it with our Rails app. This allows us to reuse all the structure we already have in Rails ecosystem, such as tests, session, authentication, and so on. Before we develop our Sinatra application, let's write an integration test.

This test should attempt to localize a date using the Polish locale but will fail because we don't have any translation data for this locale. Next, we should visit the translation URL /translator/en/pl, meaning we want to translate messages from English to Polish, fill in the appropriate translation field, and store this new translation. After that, we can assert our translation was successfully stored by being able to localize the same date. The implementation goes like this:

`translator/1_translator/test/integration/translator_app_test.rb`

```ruby
require 'test_helper'

class TranslatorAppTest < ActiveSupport::TestCase
  include Capybara

  # Clean up store and load default translations after tests
  teardown { Translator.reload! }

  test "can translate messages from a given locale to another" do
    assert_raise I18n::MissingTranslationData do
      I18n.l(Date.new(2010, 04, 17), :locale => :pl)
    end

    visit "/translator/en/pl"
    fill_in "date.formats.default", :with => %{"%d-%m-%Y"}
    click_button "Store translations"

    assert_match "Translations stored with success!", page.body
    assert_equal "17-04-2010", I18n.l(Date.new(2010, 04, 17), :locale => :pl)
  end
end
```

Since our test uses Capybara helpers, let's add Capybara to our application Gemfile:

`translator/1_translator/Gemfile`

```ruby
group :test do
  gem "capybara", "0.4.0"
end
```

And then let's configure both Capybara and our Translator.store in test/test_helper.rb:

```
translator/1_translator/test/test_helper.rb
```

```ruby
require "capybara/rails"
Rails.backtrace_cleaner.remove_silencers!
Capybara.default_driver = :rack_test
Translator.reload!
```

Notice both tests and the test/test_helper.rb files invoke a method called Translator.reload!. This method will be responsible for removing all keys from the database and reloading the translation data. Let's implement it next:

```
translator/1_translator/lib/translator.rb
```

```ruby
def self.reload!
  Translator.store.flushdb
  I18n.backend.load_translations
end
```

Now tests are ready to run with rake test:integration, but they fail because our Sinatra application is not built yet. So, let's add both Sinatra and Haml to our project Gemfile (and install these new dependencies with bundle install):

```
translator/1_translator/Gemfile
```

```ruby
gem "sinatra", "1.1.0", :require => "sinatra/base"
gem "haml", "3.0.23"
```

Our Sinatra application should define a route as /:from/:to, which, when accessed, renders a view with all translation data available in :from locale, ready to be translated to the :to locale. Our first code iteration for our Sinatra application is shown here:

```
translator/1_translator/lib/translator/app.rb
```

```ruby
require 'sinatra/base'
require 'haml'

module Translator
  class App < Sinatra::Base
    set :environment, Rails.env
    enable :inline_templates

    get "/:from/:to" do |from, to|
      exhibit_translations(from, to)
    end

    protected

    # Store from and to locales in variables and retrieve
    # all keys available for translation.
```

```ruby
    def exhibit_translations(from, to)
      @from, @to, @keys = from, to, available_keys(from)
      haml :index
    end

    # Get all keys for a locale. Remove the locale from the key and sort them.
    # If a key is named "en.foo.bar", this method will return it as "foo.bar".
    def available_keys(locale)
      keys  = Translator.store.keys("#{locale}.*")
      range = Range.new(locale.size + 1, -1)
      keys.map { |k| k.slice(range) }.sort!
    end

    # Get the value in the translator store for a given locale. This method
    # decodes values and checks if they are a hash, as we don't want subtrees
    # available for translation since they are managed automatically by I18n.
    def locale_value(locale, key)
      value = Translator.store["#{locale}.#{key}"]
      value if value && !ActiveSupport::JSON.decode(value).is_a?(Hash)
    end
  end
end
__END__

@@ index
!!!
%html
  %head
    %title
      Translator::App
  %body
    %h2= "From #{@from} to #{@to}"

    %p(style="color:green")= @message

    - if @keys.empty?
      No translations available for #{@from}
    - else
      %form(method="post" action="")
        - @keys.each do |key|
          - from_value = locale_value(@from, key)
          - next unless from_value
          - to_value = locale_value(@to, key) || from_value
          %p
            %label(for=key)
              %small= key
              = from_value
            %br
            %input(id=key name=key type="text" value=to_value size="120")
        %p
          %input(type="submit" value="Store translations")
```

There are a few things to discuss in this implementation. First, notice we explicitly forward the Rails environment to the Sinatra application one. Next, we define the /:from/:to route available through the request method GET. If a route matches, Sinatra will yield both parameters to the block, which will be executed. The block simply invokes exhibit_translations, which assigns these parameters to instance variables, gets all locale keys available for translation, and renders the index template.

In this case, we chose to use Haml[7] as template markup for the index page. The template is just a few lines of code and is in the same file as the application by using Sinatra's inline templates feature, which we enabled at the top of the application. However, it is important to notice that templates are evaluated in the same context as the application. This means any method defined in our Sinatra application, as well as its instance variables, are also available in the template. This approach is different from Rails, because Rails templates are not evaluated in the same context as controllers, but in a specific view context, so Rails needs to copy all instance variables from controllers to views behind the scenes, as we saw in Section 1.3, *Understanding Rails Rendering Stack*, on page 11, and controller methods should be called explicitly as controller.method.

Finally, notice our template calls the locale_value method. This method receives a locale and a key and returns the value stored in Redis. This method should also handle hashes, which are created and stored by default by the I18n framework, to allow you to retrieve subtrees from backends.

In I18n, whenever you store a translation { "foo.bar" => "baz" }, it decomposes the "foo.bar" key and also stores { "foo" => { "bar" => "baz"} } as the translation. This allows you to retrieve either the specific translation with I18n.t("foo.bar") #=> "bar" or a subtree hash with I18n.t("foo") #=> { "bar" => "baz" }. That said, if we show hashes in our Sinatra interface, several translations would be duplicated, because they would appear either in the subtree hash in the foo key or in the full key foo.bar.

Before we try our Sinatra application, autoload it from lib/translator.rb, as shown here:

---

7. Haml stands for HTML Abstraction Markup Language, and you can find some examples at http://haml-lang.com/.

`translator/1_translator/lib/translator.rb`

```
autoload :App, "translator/app"
```

And finally mount it in the router at "translator":

`translator/1_translator/config/routes.rb`

```
mount Translator::App, :at => "/translator"
```

Let's verify this now works by starting the server using bundle exec rails server as usual and accessing /translator/en/pl in our browser! This page automatically sets up a page to translate message from English to Polish, but don't click the submit button yet, since we still haven't implemented the POST behavior. In fact, when we run the tests again, they fail exactly for this reason. Clicking the button in integration tests causes the server to return "Not Found" instead of showing the expected success message:

```
1) Failure:
test_can_translate_messages_from_a_given_locale_to_another(TranslatorAppTest)
  <"Not Found"> expected to be =~
</Translations\ stored\ with\ success!/>.
```

To make the test pass, let's add a new route to Sinatra for POST requests. This new route should store the translation in the I18n backend, passing the destination locale and the translations decoded from JSON to Ruby; call save in the Redis store, forcing it to be dumped to the filesystem; and exhibit the translation page once again:

`translator/2_final/lib/translator/app.rb`

```
post "/:from/:to" do |from, to|
  I18n.backend.store_translations to, decoded_translations, :escape => false
  Translator.store.save
  @message = "Translations stored with success!"
  exhibit_translations(from, to)
end


protected

# Get all translations sent through the form and decode
# their JSON values to check validity.
def decoded_translations
  translations = params.except("from", "to")
  translations.each do |key, value|
    translations[key] = ActiveSupport::JSON.decode(value) rescue nil
  end
end
```

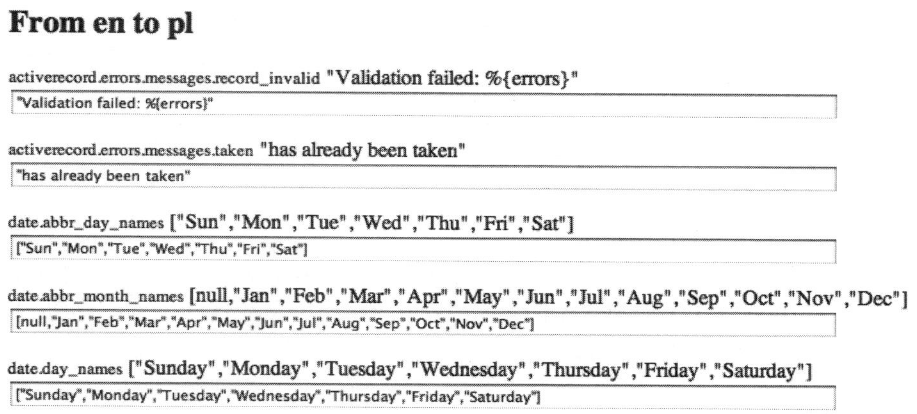

From en to pl

activerecord.errors.messages.record_invalid "Validation failed: %{errors}"

"Validation failed: %{errors}"

activerecord.errors.messages.taken "has already been taken"

"has already been taken"

date.abbr_day_names ["Sun","Mon","Tue","Wed","Thu","Fri","Sat"]

["Sun","Mon","Tue","Wed","Thu","Fri","Sat"]

date.abbr_month_names [null,"Jan","Feb","Mar","Apr","May","Jun","Jul","Aug","Sep","Oct","Nov","Dec"]

[null,"Jan","Feb","Mar","Apr","May","Jun","Jul","Aug","Sep","Oct","Nov","Dec"]

date.day_names ["Sunday","Monday","Tuesday","Wednesday","Thursday","Friday","Saturday"]

["Sunday","Monday","Tuesday","Wednesday","Thursday","Friday","Saturday"]

Figure 7.1: TRANSLATOR APP

Notice we set :escape to **false** when storing translations so I18n can properly generate subtrees. By default, if you give a translation as { "foo.bar" => "baz" }, I18n will treat it as a single key, escaped as { "foo\000.bar" => "baz" }. When it's stored this way, we cannot retrieve its subtree as I18n.t("foo"). However, if we turn escaping to false, I18n will break the key apart, converting it to { "foo" => { "bar" => "baz" } } and allow us to retrieve it as I18n.t("foo") or as I18n.t("foo.bar").

Feel free to restart the server and translate all data from any locale to another! Notice we choose to represent the data as JSON in the interface, because we can easily represent arrays, strings, numbers, or booleans. At this point, all our tests are green as well!

We will come back to our Translator application and add a couple more features soon, but first, let's take a closer look at the Rails 3 router.

7.4 Understanding the Rails Router

In Rails 3, the router's API and backend were reimplemented in order to better integrate with Rack. It allows us to map any route to a Rack application:

```
Rails.application.routes.draw do
  match "/hello", :to =>
    lambda { |env| [200, { "Content-Type" => "text/html" }, ["World"]] }
end
```

When we add this route to any Rails application and hit /hello in the browser, we get "World" as the response from the server. In fact, when you have a route like this:

```
Rails.application.routes.draw do
  match "/hello", :to => "posts#index"
end
```

Rails, before a request, automatically converts controller#action to a Rack application. You can retrieve any action from a controller as a Rack application by simply doing this:

```
PostsController.action(:index)
PostsController.action(:index).responds_to?(:call) # => true
```

When we look at the source code for the action method, we can see Rails generates a Rack application on demand and wraps it around the controller middleware stack we discussed in Section 5.3, *Middleware Stacks*, on page 98. This Rack application simply initializes a controller and invokes the dispatch method, passing the action name to be processed and a request object as parameters:

```
rails/actionpack/lib/action_controller/metal.rb
class ActionController::Metal < AbstractController::Base
  # Creates a Rack application on the fly that
  # dispatches the given action name.
  def self.action(name, klass = ActionDispatch::Request)
    middleware_stack.build(name.to_s) do |env|
      new.dispatch(name, klass.new(env))
    end
  end

  # Dispatches the given action name by processing it
  # and returning a valid Rack response.
  def dispatch(name, request)
    @_request = request
    @_env = request.env
    @_env['action_controller.instance'] = self
    process(name)
    to_a
  end

  def to_a
    [status, headers, response_body]
  end
end
```

Whenever you call get, post, put, delete, resources, or resource in the new router DSL, at the end they always call the match method. The only method that has different semantics, is mount, used earlier in this chapter to mount our Sinatra application.

The match method works by generating a regular expression that matches exactly the given route. When you say match "/translator", it only matches paths as /^\/translator$/ (the query string is not considered in matches). However, when mounting a Sinatra application, we don't want to match just /translator but also /translator/en/pl, /translator/foo/bar, and so on. In other words, what we really want is the generated regular expression to be /^\/translator/, without "$" as anchor. And this is exactly what the mount method does.

You may have noticed there is something more going on. If any requests to /translator/en/pl are being handled by Sinatra but we have only /:from/:to as a route declared in Sinatra, how is Sinatra able to match them?

Whenever a request hits a server, the server gets the request path and sends it as ENV["PATH_INFO"] to the Rack application. Mounting applications works because, when dispatching the request to Sinatra, Rails removes /translator from env["PATH_INFO"], so Sinatra only sees /en/pl (as if the browser were accessing /en/pl straight in the Sinatra application).

All this is outlined in the Rack specification, which also specifies that Rails should set env["SCRIPT_NAME"] = "/translator" in order to tell Sinatra that it is mounted in a specific point, in case Sinatra wants to use this information.

The router in Rails 3 is a perfect example of the flexibility that can be achieved with Rack, and there is still much more to be improved. For example, could authentication or testing frameworks enjoy this flexibility? Certainly! And luckily, a few frameworks in the community already do it. This is what we are going to check out next!

7.5 Taking It to the Next Level with Devise and Capybara

If any of our applications are going to provide an interface for translations, we should make sure this interface is password-protected and that we can properly test its functionality. In this section, let's take a look at Devise,[8] a full-stack authentication solution based on Rack, and a deeper look at how Capybara[9] can be used to test Rack applications.

Adding Cross-Application Authentication

Devise is an interesting solution for authentication because it provides, in very few lines of code, a whole authentication stack, with sign-in, sign-up, password recovery, and more. It uses Warden[10] to move the authentication handling to the middleware stack, allowing any application, regardless if it is Sinatra or a Rails controller, to use the same authentication rules.

To add Devise to our Translator app, we first need to add it to your Gemfile and call Bundler to install it:

`translator/2_final/Gemfile`

```
gem "devise", "1.1.3"
```

With the gem installed in our machine, we need to invoke the devise:install generator:

```
bundle exec rails g devise:install
```

The generator copies a locale file and a initializer with several configuration options to our application. At the end, it also prints some steps that we need to do manually.

The first one is to configure Action Mailer for development:

`translator/2_final/config/environments/development.rb`

```
config.action_mailer.default_url_options = { :host => 'localhost:3000' }
```

Then add flash messages to our layout:

`translator/2_final/app/views/layouts/application.html.erb`

```
<p class="notice"><%= notice %></p>
<p class="alert"><%= alert %></p>
```

And finally add a root route:

`translator/2_final/config/routes.rb`

```
root :to => "home#index"
```

---

8. https://github.com/plataformatec/devise
9. https://github.com/jnicklas/capybara
10. https://github.com/hassox/warden

Since our root route points to a HomeController, let's implement it as well. For now, the index action simply renders a link to the mounted Sinatra application:

translator/2_final/app/controllers/home_controller.rb

```
class HomeController < ApplicationController
  def index
    render :inline =>
      "<%= link_to 'Translate from English to Polish', '/translator/en/pl' %>"
  end
end
```

With all of the setup done, we are ready to create our first Devise model, called Admin:

```
bundle exec rails g devise Admin
```

And then run the migration added by the generator:

```
rake db:migrate
```

At this point, we didn't make any significant change to our application, but if we run our integration tests, they will fail. This is because Rails is trying to load fixtures for our integration test. Let's disable it by removing fixtures :all from ActiveSupport::TestCase at test/test_helper.rb. Also, since we defined a root route, let's remove the default public/index.html file as well.

With integration tests passing once again, let's fire up a new server, visit /admins/sign_up, create a new admin account, and sign in. You can also access /admins/edit if you want to change your account (although you may want to disable this sign-up ability before deploying the app).

Devise provides several helpers to restrict access to your Rails controllers. Since we created a model called Admin, we can use authenticate_admin! as a before filter, and the request proceeds only if an admin model is authenticated:

```
class PostsController < ApplicationController
  before_filter :authenticate_admin!
end
```

However, we want to add authentication to our Sinatra app, where Devise does not include any helpers. Fortunately, this is still trivial to achieve with Devise because of Warden. Whenever we invoke authenticate_admin! in a Rails controller, it simply executes the following:

```
env["warden"].authenticate!(:scope => "admin")
```

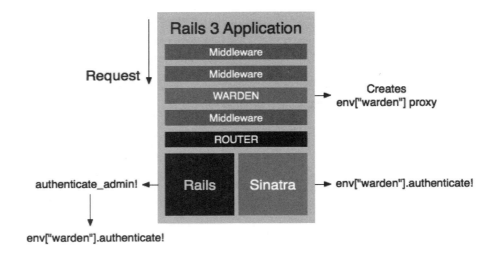

Figure 7.2: The middleware stack and Rack applications involved in a request to a Rails 3 app with Sinatra, Warden, and Devise

The env["warden"] object used previously is a proxy created by the Warden middleware, and this middleware is added by Devise to the Rails middleware stack using a Rails::Engine, just as we did in Section 5.3, *MuteMiddleware*, on page 101. Since this middleware is executed before hitting the router, the proxy object is also available in Sinatra, and we can easily add authentication to Translator::App in a before filter:

`translator/2_final/lib/translator/app.rb`

```
before do
  env["warden"].authenticate!(:scope => "admin")
end
```

Now when you request the Sinatra application without an admin signed in, the previous before filter will throw an error. This error is caught by the Warden middleware using Ruby's *throw/catch* syntax and allowing Warden to redirect you to the sign-in page inside Devise. Once you sign in, the previous code will simply return the current admin in session, proceeding with Sinatra request.

Although this approach allows us to use the same authentication mechanism across different Rack applications, it has one issue: it requires us to change the Sinatra application by adding a before filter. That said, if we are using a third-party Sinatra application, like the one provided in the Resque[11] gem, we won't be able to modify it.

In this case, we could ensure authentication at the router level, without a need to change the Sinatra application, as shown here:

```
authenticate "admin" do
  mount Translator::App, :at => "/translator"
end
```

The authenticate shown previously is added by Devise to the Rails router, and it simply uses the router's constraint API to ensure the "admin" role is authenticated. Let's check its implementation in Devise source code:

```
def authenticate(scope)
  constraint = lambda do |request|
    request.env["warden"].authenticate!(:scope => scope)
  end

  constraints(constraint) do
    yield
  end
end
```

Regardless if we choose a before filter or a router constraint to require authentication in our Sinatra application, we can check the translator backend is now secure by rerunning our test suite and watching it fail.

```
1) Error:
test_can_translate_messages_from_a_given_locale_to_another(TranslatorAppTest)
  Capybara::ElementNotFound: cannot fill in, no text field, text area or
password field with id, name, or label 'date.formats.default' found
```

The test cannot find the "date.formats.default" label given to fill_in because it is showing the /admin/sign_in page instead of the translations page. To fix it, let's authenticate an admin in our integration test using a setup hook:

`translator/2_final/test/integration/translator_app_test.rb`

```
setup { sign_in(admin) }

def admin
  @admin ||= Admin.create!(
    :email => "admin_#{Admin.count}@example.org",
    :password => "123456"
  )
end
```

---

11. https://github.com/defunkt/resque

```
def sign_in(admin)
  visit "/admins/sign_in"
  fill_in "Email",    :with => admin.email
  fill_in "Password", :with => admin.password
  click_button "Sign in"
end
```

With this setup, let's run our test suite again and watch it pass! Notice we decided to manually sign the admin in by filling out the form, instead of using a hack in our tests that modifies the session or passes in a cookie. In fact, even if we wanted to modify the session or a cookie, Capybara would not allow us to do that. And, as we will see next, it actually has a great reason to not allow this.

Adding Cross-Browser Testing

When we go back and check the code created with enginex in any of the previous chapters, we notice that, for our integration tests, enginex creates an ActiveSupport::IntegrationCase class instead of using Action-Controller::IntegrationTest:

```
# Define a bare test case to use with Capybara
class ActiveSupport::IntegrationCase < ActiveSupport::TestCase
  include Capybara
  include Rails.application.routes.url_helpers
end
```

While writing Rails integration tests using ActionController::IntegrationTest, we have full access to the raw request and response objects, allowing us to check and manipulate cookies, sessions, headers, and so on. Capybara, on the other hand, has a very closed API that does not expose these. That said, if we simply included Capybara in Action-Controller::IntegrationTest, we would be tempted to access and manipulate these objects, leading to both conceptual and practical issues.

Let's discuss the conceptual issue a bit. Capybara was designed to let us write integration tests from the mind-set of an end user. For example, imagine we are building an ecommerce site that keeps the last five products we viewed in the footer. If our implementation is simply storing these product IDs in the session, a naive integration test would simply assert that, after accessing a product page, the product ID was added to the session.

The issue with this kind of test is that the ecommerce user does not care at all if something was stored in the session. They just want to

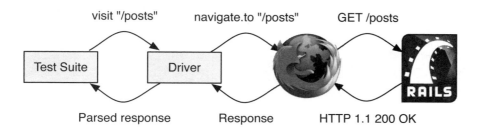

Figure 7.3: CALL TRACE WHEN USING CAPYBARA WITH SELENIUM DRIVER
AND FIREFOX

see the last-visited products in the footer and be able to click them,
something we did not assert in our tests.

Besides, the fact we store this information in the session is an implementation detail. If at some point we decide to keep this data in a
cookie, our naive test will fail, while it should still pass since the user
interface has not changed at all. This is a common symptom in tests
too coupled to their implementation.

For this reason, Capybara hides all these internals from you, which
works out well considering that one of the most important features in
Capybara is that it supports different drivers. Except for the Rack test
driver, which is Ruby-specific and accesses a Rack application directly,
Capybara drivers manipulate a browser, which then accesses our application through a web server. Some drivers such as as Selenium use
common browsers as Mozilla Firefox, Internet Explorer, and Google
Chrome, while others interact with a headless browser like HtmlUnit
and EnvJS.

As you may expect, each browser supported by Selenium must expose a
limited API. Some may expose access to cookies; others may not. Some
headless browsers may give you full control on request headers, but
others do not. To allow you to switch drivers and browsers without a
need to rewrite a huge part of your integration tests, Capybara focuses
on the common set supported by most of them.

By default, Capybara uses Rack::Test, which is the same library used
by Rails 3 integration tests and does not require our application to be
exposed through a web server. But we can easily change our Translator

application tests to use Selenium[12] by adding the following lines to our test helper:

`translator/2_final/test/test_helper.rb`

```ruby
require "selenium-webdriver"
# Can be :chrome, :firefox or :ie
Selenium::WebDriver.for :firefox
Capybara.default_driver = :selenium

class ActiveSupport::TestCase
  # Disable transactional fixtures for integration testing
  self.use_transactional_fixtures = false
end
```

Selenium uses real browsers to test our application. By default it uses Firefox,[13] which you need to have installed before running tests again. After you install it, run our integration tests again, and notice that Selenium is automatically starting Firefox and driving it against our website! At the end, our tests still pass!

Because Selenium needs to access a web server for each request, Capybara automatically starts one up. Since Capybara fires this new web server in a thread, the database connection used in tests is not the same used by the server in each request. That said, if we use transactional fixtures to wrap each test in a database transaction, the data created in tests won't be available in the server since transactional data is not shared between database connections until it is committed. This is the reason we need to disable transactional fixtures in our test/test_helper.rb file, even though it reduces performance.

Another consequence of disabling transactional fixtures is that the data stored in our database is not cleaned up between tests, and this will definitely get in the way as we add new tests to our suite. Fortunately, a few solutions are already available today that do all this work for us. One that stands out is Database Cleaner,[14] since it supports different ORMs and databases.

7.6 Wrapping Up

In this chapter, we created another Rails application and used the opportunity to better describe how Rails applications are structured

---

12. http://seleniumhq.org/
13. http://www.mozilla.com/firefox/
14. https://github.com/bmabey/database_cleaner

and designed. We discussed the importance of the Rack specification and how it makes easy for different frameworks (such as Rails and Sinatra) to play along without hassle. We also learned more about I18n, its backends, and its extensions. Plus, we found and implemented a good case to use a simple key-value store as Redis.

At the end, we discussed two gems that are widely used in the Rails community: Devise and Capybara. Even though it was simply an introduction, I advise you to take the next step and play with them a bit more. And by playing, I mean not only using them but checking out their source code. You will see how Devise uses ActionController::Metal, as we saw in Section 3.3, *Playing with Metal*, on page 59, to define a bare-bones controller and learn how Capybara makes use of Rack applications and handlers to automatically start up servers.

That finishes our tour of Rails 3. Everything we discussed (the rendering stack, railties, engines, generators, Active Model, and so on) are not only powerful APIs for the development of Rails extensions and applications but also for the development of Rails itself. We can definitely expect more powerful engines and more Active Model modules in upcoming Rails releases.

While developing your next web application or maintaining an existing one, remember all the tools available to make your code cleaner. You can use responders to DRY up your controller and use generators to keep you and your team productive. You are also able to analyze other Rails extensions source code, submit changes, and debug problems with more ease.

Finally, you understand Rails better. You can explore other areas of the source code, study other Action Controller and Active Models modules, check other generators implementations, or read the source of railties, engines, and applications with detail! Rails also has detailed guides on how to contribute to Rails,[15] so if you haven't yet, this is the high time to propose improvements or fix some bugs that may have bothered you some time ago.

I hope this book has taught you new ways to improve your Ruby code and Rails applications. Most of all, I hope you had fun.

—José Valim

---

15. http://guides.rubyonrails.org/contributing_to_rails.html

Index

More from PragProg.com

SQL Antipatterns

If you're programming applications that store data, then chances are you're using SQL, either directly or through a mapping layer. But most of the SQL that gets used is inefficient, hard to maintain, and sometimes just plain wrong. This book shows you all the common mistakes, and then leads you through the best fixes. What's more, it shows you what's *behind* these fixes, so you'll learn a lot about relational databases along the way.

SQL Antipatterns: Avoiding the Pitfalls of Database Programming
Bill Karwin
(300 pages) ISBN: 978-19343565-5-5. $34.95
http://pragprog.com/titles/bksqla

Seven Languages in Seven Weeks

In this book you'll get a hands-on tour of Clojure, Haskell, Io, Prolog, Scala, Erlang, and Ruby. Whether or not your favorite language is on that list, you'll broaden your perspective of programming by examining these languages side-by-side. You'll learn something new from each, and best of all, you'll learn how to learn a language quickly.

Seven Languages in Seven Weeks: A Pragmatic Guide to Learning Programming Languages
Bruce A. Tate
(300 pages) ISBN: 978-1934356-59-3. $34.95
http://pragprog.com/titles/btlang

More from PragProg.com

Driving Technical Change

Your co-workers' resistance to new technologies can be baffling. Learn to read users' "patterns of resistance"—and then dismantle their objections. Every developer must master the art of evangelizing. With these techniques and strategies, you'll help your organization adopt your solutions—without selling your soul to organizational politics.

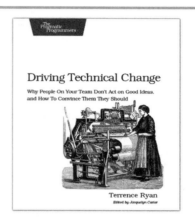

Driving Technical Change: Why People On Your Team Don't Act On Good Ideas, and How to Convince Them They Should
Terrence Ryan
(200 pages) ISBN: 978-1934356-60-9. $32.95
http://pragprog.com/titles/trevan

Agile in a Flash

The best agile book isn't a book: Agile in a Flash is a unique deck of index cards that fit neatly in your pocket. You can tape them to the wall. Spread them out on your project table. Get stains on them over lunch. These cards are meant to be used, not just read.

Agile in a Flash: Speed-Learning Agile Software Development
Jeff Langr and Tim Ottinger
(110 pages) ISBN: 978-1-93435-671-5. $15.00
http://pragprog.com/titles/olag

The Pragmatic Bookshelf

The Pragmatic Bookshelf features books written by developers for developers. The titles continue the well-known Pragmatic Programmer style and continue to garner awards and rave reviews. As development gets more and more difficult, the Pragmatic Programmers will be there with more titles and products to help you stay on top of your game.

Visit Us Online

Home Page for "Crafting Rails Applications"
http://pragprog.com/titles/jvrails
Source code from this book, errata, and other resources. Come give us feedback, too!

Register for Updates
http://pragprog.com/updates
Be notified when updates and new books become available.

Join the Community
http://pragprog.com/community
Read our weblogs, join our online discussions, participate in our mailing list, interact with our wiki, and benefit from the experience of other Pragmatic Programmers.

New and Noteworthy
http://pragprog.com/news
Check out the latest pragmatic developments, new titles and other offerings.

Save on the eBook

Save on the eBook versions of this title. Owning the paper version of this book entitles you to purchase the electronic versions at a terrific discount.

PDFs are great for carrying around on your laptop—they are hyperlinked, have color, and are fully searchable. Most titles are also available for the iPhone and iPod touch, Amazon Kindle, and other popular e-book readers.

Buy now at pragprog.com/coupon.

Contact Us

Online Orders: www.pragprog.com/catalog
Customer Service: support@pragprog.com
Non-English Versions: translations@pragprog.com
Pragmatic Teaching: academic@pragprog.com
Author Proposals: proposals@pragprog.com
Contact us: 1-800-699-PROG (+1 919 847 3884)